PLAUTUS:
THE DARKER
COMEDIES

D1018557

Jack O'Connell

Seattle

29 décembre 1983

PLAUTUS: THE DARKER COMEDIES

Bacchides, Casina, and Truculentus

Translated from the Latin,
with Introduction and Notes,
by James Tatum

THE JOHNS HOPKINS UNIVERSITY PRESS
Baltimore and London

This book has been brought to publication with the
generous assistance of the David M. Robinson Publication
Fund and of the Faculty of Arts and Sciences, Dartmouth
College.

© 1983 by The Johns Hopkins University Press
All rights reserved
Printed in the United States of America

The Johns Hopkins University Press, Baltimore, Maryland 21218
The Johns Hopkins Press Ltd, London

Library of Congress Cataloging in Publication Data

Plautus, Titus Maccius.
  Plautus, the darker comedies.
  Contents: Bacchides—Casina—Truculentus.
  I. Tatum, James   II. Title.
PA6570.A3   1983   872'.01   82–21160
ISBN   0–8018–2900–3
ISBN   0–8018–2901–1 (pbk.)

FOR BILL COOK

. . .et serves animae dimidium meae

CONCORDIA UNIVERSITY LIBRARY
PORTLAND, OR 97211

CONTENTS

PREFACE

The three comedies in this collection are revised scripts from productions at Dartmouth of *Bacchides* (1981), *Casina* (1977), and *Truculentus* (1976). Actors and director played an important role at every stage of translation, production, and revision. I am indebted first of all to a loyal troupe of performers who contributed much to my own sense of how Plautus's comedies can work as plays in the theater. In effect, they became a repertory company, one perhaps not so very different in spirit from the *grex* (herd) with whom Plautus acted and for whom he wrote. Among those who helped bring these versions to life for the first time, I should especially like to thank Peter Saccio (Diniarchus in *Truculentus*, Lysidamus in *Casina*, Nicobulus in *Bacchides*), Bonnie Wallin (Phronesium in *Truculentus*, Pardalisca in *Casina*, Bacchis of Athens in *Bacchides*), Helen Dunlop (Astaphium in *Truculentus,* Cleostrata in *Casina*), Sharon Washington (Myrrhina in *Casina*), Priscilla Sears (Bacchis of Samos in *Bacchides*), Laurence Davies (Chrysalus in *Bacchides*), Nathan Hine (Alcesimus in *Casina*), Evan Haley (Truculentus in *Truculentus*), Oliver Taplin (Lydus in *Bacchides*), Henry Buckley (Stratophanes in *Truculentus*), and Mark Molloy (Pistoclerus in *Bacchides*). I am also grateful to the memory of Cory Fifield (Olympio in *Casina*), whose career in the theater was cut short at twenty-four by leukemia. All these voices and characterizations remained vividly in my memory long after production. In most places the actors' way of playing a scene is preserved in the stage directions. Sometimes only their struggle with lines in performance made me realize that what I had given them to speak did not work. As with most scripts, more such lines doubtless remain even now.

Robert Connor first suggested to me such a collaborative venture. In retrospect the enterprise seems an obvious one to have undertaken. Cynthia Dessen encouraged me to aim for production of *Truculentus* and, afterwards, to persevere in the translation and production of the other two plays rather than of the more popular (and safer) comedies of Plautus. Oliver Taplin, William Arrowsmith, Douglass Parker, Amy Richlin, Catharine Chapman, Jack Harvey, Christine Perkell, and Niall Slater offered helpful comments on many aspects of the manuscript. Joanne Allen was most helpful in the hectic business of revising and editing the final copy. I am once again grateful to Catherine Frasier for typing the drafts of the scripts and the final copy. In the Charybdis of a departmental office she maintained good cheer even when confronted with a page that had to be retyped for the tenth time.

My greatest debt is to William W. Cook, of the Dartmouth English Department. He directed all three productions and was an indispensable collaborator from the first line of *Truculentus*'s prologue down to the epilogue of the *Bacchides*. His wide knowledge of comedy and farce can be detected on nearly every page of these translations. He helped to make the unspeakable speakable and, just as often, where Plautus demanded it, the speakable appropriately unspeakable.

INTRODUCTION

THE PLAYWRIGHT AND HIS WORLD

Our knowledge of the literary history of Greece and Rome often depends on little evidence.[1] In the case of Titus Maccius Plautus that evidence is particularly meager, anecdotal, and suspect. He seems to have stood still scarcely long enough to write down the lines of his comedies. Like one of his own harried characters, he ran across the stage of Roman life and literature, from some point in the latter half of the third century B.C. until perhaps 183 B.C. After many years of intensive research, we know less than we would like to know about him and the conventions of his theater: less, for example, than we know about the stagecraft of Aeschylus, Sophocles, Euripides, or Aristophanes.[2]

Plautus based his comedies on Greek New Comedy of the fourth and third centuries B.C.—"new," that is, in relation to the Old Comedy of the fifth century B.C. The greatest poet of all was Menander of Athens (ca. 342–291 B.C.). He and others wrote for a city transformed from the democracy of Thucydides and Aristophanes. Unhappily, save for his only complete play, *Dyskolos* (*The Grouch*), or a long fragment like *Samia* (*The Woman from Samos*), Greek New Comedy survives only in fragments.[3] Enough remains to show that we would search through them in vain for echoes of the kind of momentous political and social upheavals so vividly reflected in comedies like Aristophanes' *Clouds* or *Lysistrata*. Menander was celebrated in antiquity for being an unrivaled student of the human comedy. As the saying went, "O Menander and Life, which of you imitated the other?" His subjects were the politics of the family, the desires and the intrigues of fathers, sons, mothers, daughters, slaves, and courtesans, not genuine political figures of the magnitude of Pericles.[4] For us today New Comedy may seem tame compared with the liberal imagination and fantasy of Aristophanic comedy. But in antiquity, when he existed in his entirety rather than in his parts, Menander was regarded as a poet equal to Homer and superior to Aristophanes himself.[5]

In Plautus's hands this already politically discrete theater became doubly removed from the arena of public politics and controversy. His plays are never set in Rome, but rather in some Greek city, often, as with *Bacchides, Casina,* and *Truculentus,* in Athens itself. With the exception of a few characters who have Latin names, such as Truculentus, the casts are made up of persons at least nominally Greek. There are occasionally topical allusions, as when a supposedly Greek slave makes fun of the city of Praeneste outside Rome (*Truculentus* III.2), but these local in jokes are rare and funny precisely because they break the dramatic illusion of a play set in Greece. What results on the stage is a free, vaguely Greek world which is at the same time thoroughly Roman in its outlook and, of course, Latin-speaking. Together with Terence (ca. 195–159 B.C.), his only successor at Rome, Plautus exercised enormous influence on theater in the West. Lope de Vega, Shakespeare, Jonson, Molière, Dryden, Kleist, and Giraudoux all reveal Plautus's influence in their comedies, either by direct imitation of a particular play or, sometimes, by adapting Plautus's dramatic techniques for their own purposes.

Since the kind of open theater which Euripides or Aristophanes enjoyed was never welcome at Rome, even the most assiduous reading between the lines of Plautus has yielded frustratingly little new information about the political situation of his day.[6] The plays also reveal little about Plautus himself. One of our few "facts" is that he made a living out of his comedies, probably as much by being an actor and director of his *grex* (herd or troupe of actors) as by being a playwright. Hence the prologue's hope in *Casina* for our well-being and our entertainment. These are more than conventional pleasantries: they are there because Plautus depended on audiences for his livelihood.

Serene as they are about serious matters of national politics, Plautus's comedies provided popular entertainment for a generation of Romans who were themselves anything but serene. His lifetime spanned an age in which Rome fought one bitter war after another with Greeks, Carthaginians, and any other nation that stood in the way of what came to be seen, in hindsight, as an inevitable rise to mastery of the Mediterranean world. The devastation caused by the Second Punic War with Hannibal was the greatest threat Rome ever faced, and it was for a nation locked in such life-and-death struggles that Plautus wrote his comedies.[7] His plays were designed for performance on those festival days which afforded the leisure (*otium*) for relaxation from the Romans' usual regimen of hard work and business, that daily routine they interestingly termed *negotium*, "not leisure time."[8] The Hellenophile Simone Weil, no friend of Roman civilization, has suggested that Plautus's mordant, cynical comedy appealed to a well-developed national taste for cruelty, whether on the stage or in real life.[9]

Of all Rome's neighbors, the Greeks nonetheless resisted with the most ingenuity, and not in the way a Roman general or statesman could have anticipated. As Horace was later to put it, the rude conquerors became themselves captives of the Greece they had conquered. While the Italians had their own native poetic and dramatic forms, such as the *fabulae Atellanae* (popular farce) and *fabula togata* (comedy in native dress), such indigenous literary efforts counted as nothing in the face of the overwhelming influence of the Greeks. Latin literature was completely transformed by the Greeks, and this transformation was well under way during Plautus's lifetime.

The process of adapting Greek literature to the Latin language and Roman ways was complex. From the first it was far more than simple translation, though that task in itself was difficult enough. Plautus and other Roman authors in effect added a new chapter to the history of every literary genre the Greeks had invented.

We do not know how many plays Plautus wrote and produced. By the end of the first century B.C. over 130 were attributed to him. At that point the Augustan scholar Varro attempted to establish an authentic canon of Plautine comedy; he arrived at a list of twenty-one plays. The same number of comedies survived the vicissitudes to which all ancient texts were subject. Possibly but not certainly the plays we have are the same ones Varro approved.

THE PLAYS IN THIS VOLUME

Anyone familiar with Plautus's most popular plays might wonder what to expect of a collection of his "darker comedies." By this title I mean to suggest that this is not a random collection. The three comedies are unconventional in plot and in morals. They are uncompromisingly derisive of the family and of the conventional uses of love. Their endings offer no redemption and no return to an easy social order. They were probably all produced late in Plautus's career. Each of them suffered considerable damage in the transmission of texts from the ancient world.

While many of Plautus's comedies depict a comic inversion of society, with slaves the masters and masters the slaves, *Bacchides*, *Casina*, and *Truculentus* go well beyond our usual expectations of Roman comedy. The cheerful resolution of *Miles Gloriosus* or *Menaechmi* seems all apple-cheeked innocence by comparison. In *Truculentus* the courtesan Phronesium and her maid Astaphium snare all four of the men they set out to catch, and take all their money in the bargain. In the finale of *Bacchides* the sisters Bacchis succeed in persuading two fathers to join their own sons in the same bed. The cast of characters in *Casina* is more domestic, but the play is not more respectable. Unambiguous scenes of transvestism and homosexuality offended at least one member of every audience to which the comedy was played, and sometimes many more than one. Everywhere there is an acid tone to the humor: there is not one pair of amiable young lovers, no courtesan with a heart of gold, no old man of decent or kindly disposition. *Bacchides* and *Truculentus* do not conform to the conventions of New Comedy which Northrop Frye speaks of in *The Anatomy of Criticism*:

> The plot structure of Greek New Comedy as transmitted by Plautus and Terence, in itself less a form than a formula, has become the basis for most comedy especially in its more highly conventionalized dramatic form, down to our own day. . . . What normally happens is that a young man wants a young woman, that his desire is resisted by some opposition, usually paternal, and that near the end of the play some twist in the plot enables the hero to have his will. In this simple pattern there are several complex elements. In the first place, the movement of comedy is usually a movement from one kind of society to another. At the beginning of the play the obstructing characters are in charge of the play's society, and the audience recognizes that they are usurpers. At the end of the play the device in the plot that brings hero and heroine together causes a new society to crystallize around the hero,

and the moment when this crystallization occurs is the point of resolution in the action, the comic discovery, *anagnoresis* or *cognitio*.[10]

There are no heroines or heroes to be seen in *Bacchides* or *Truculentus*, at least none in the ordinary sense of those words. *Casina* comes the closest of the three to resembling the "barrier comedy" which Frye describes, since the old man Lysidamus does try to steal his son's bride on her wedding day. In the end, he is thwarted by his wife Cleostrata. But Plautus is more interested in Lysidamus and his humiliation than in young love. The hero and heroine (Casina and Euthynicus), traditionally the center of the plot of New Comedy, never even appear on the stage. Plautus's more familiar comedies are better known in no small part because they are more conventional in their plot and in their resolution. A comedy like *Miles Gloriosus* could serve as a text for secondary school, for example, and so it has for a very long time. It is still hard to imagine *Casina*, *Bacchides*, or *Truculentus* serving in the same capacity.

THE ORIGINAL TEXT

Aside from the cynical morals and unconventional plots, the most serious obstacle to a wider audience has undoubtedly been the condition of the Latin text. The special problem of textual criticism does not require much comment here, but by way of a more objective balance to the above remarks about these three comedies, it should at least be mentioned in passing.

The transmission of any text from the ancient world was always a precarious business, and of no author was this truer than of Plautus. Even his most popular comedies, the ones which survived intact in manuscripts, present the scholar with hundreds of puzzling constructions, possible interpolations, spurious readings, or just plain nonsense. Many of these textual problems are not yet solved, and may never be. These three plays very nearly did not survive at all. The opening of *Bacchides* is almost entirely lost, as is much of the closing scene of *Casina*. *Truculentus* has problems everywhere; it is the most damaged of all the complete comedies which survive, with fully one-third of the text from its manuscripts lost or muddled beyond repair. Only the labors of many textual critics and other translators made it possible to think of attempting new translations and productions.[11] More detailed comments about each play's text will be found below, in the notes to each translation.

THE TRANSLATIONS

Although much in each English play is close to the original Latin, these versions were never conceived as line-by-line translations to the letter. They are memoirs of performances, production scripts designed to give the reader a sense of the actual theatrical experience of Plautus's comedies. Each version was from the first oriented to production, and in their final form they proceed from production. I have tried everywhere to face the necessity of bringing across a scene on the stage. Essential blocking is in the text, either implicitly in the lines or in the stage directions. The most important consideration for me was to find a principal word or line in a given sequence which would make a scene work on the stage, in English. Very often this entailed singling out only one of several levels in Plautus's Latin, at the expense of others. Some of the more radical departures from a literal version are discussed in the notes.

Translating for actors poses special problems.[12] While footnotes work well enough in a text that is only to be read, they cannot dance across the stage during a performance. Plautus's exuberant language is a constant flow of puns, parodies, and other kinds of wordplay, above all alliteration. Actors need equivalent effects in the lines they speak as much as they need the sense of the original. One feature peculiar to Plautine comedy requires special comment. *Bacchides, Casina,* and *Truculentus* are plays in which the spoken dialogue frequently alternates with passages in elaborately varied rhythms, originally for what was probably chanted song or recitative. Such a passage is traditionally called the *canticum* (in the plural *cantica*). In general, directors and actors will find that the *cantica* vary the pace of action and heighten important moments in a play. Because of the *cantica,* Plautus has often been compared to Gilbert and Sullivan or Rogers and Hammerstein, as if he were a writer of musical comedy. The analogy is in fact misleading.[13] We know very little about how the *cantica* were performed in Plautus's day, save that there was at least a flute player on stage with the actors. We know even less about Roman music itself, although it is clear that the instruments at hand would have been simpler than any combination in use in a modern theater. One point must be stressed:

cantica are not show tunes like "You coax the blues right out of the horn, Mame. / You charm the husk right off of the corn, Mame" or patter songs like "When I was a lad I served a term / as office boy to an attorney's firm." Unlike the strophe and antistrophe of choruses in Greek tragedies, they do not unfold in regular stanzas, but in sequences in which the verse can change meter from one line to the next.[14] Nor is their language the language of lyric poetry. They are immensely varied; by turns parodic, explosively alliterative, they always raise ordinary dialogue to a more rhetorical and artificial level.

For a modern production, a balance has to be struck between two extremes. The *cantica* should not be rendered as normal speech, since this would result in a flatter and blander script than Plautus intended. Neither should they invariably be turned into something which I think would be alien to the nature of many *cantica*, the show tune of a Broadway musical. My solution was to translate the *cantica* to give actors and directors an opportunity for a variety of theatrical effects. Some seemed to work best as passages to be sung, with or without musical accompaniment; others were blocked out as dance or mime; still others only as soliloquy. The aim of this heuristic approach was to construct theatrical events. This is what the *cantica* must be: spectacular scenes.

A word of warning is also in order about the lines. They will not always seem natural or easy to speak. They are not easy to read in Plautus's Latin. The mellifluous elegance which a poet of the later Republic or the Augustan age favored was not always Plautus's concern; nor is this to his discredit. Actors or readers must be ready to deliver bombastic speeches like the orations of the braggart warrior Stratophanes (*Truculentus* II.6), the stuttering, alliterative lines of the slave Chrysalus when he is confronted with the soldier Cleomachus (*Bacchides* IV.8), or the "mad scene" of Pardalisca (*Casina* III.5) as if they were the most normal way in the world for one human being to speak to another. The exuberant language reflects the enormous energy of the comedy itself.

PRODUCTION

When Plautus is produced today, much will depend on the resources at hand. To re-create an authentic performance in the style of his original productions remains an ideal beyond our reach.[15]

Whatever those first performances were like, they took place in a setting far more modest than anything an archaeological ruin of an ancient theater might suggest. Plautus rarely had such monuments to perform in. His theater was more likely a cleared space with a narrow stage. Modern production of his comedies can succeed with comparatively simple sets, costumes, and technical support. Some care must be given to the choice of theater. Small, intimate halls and theaters in the round should be avoided. Such spaces tend to restrict the movement of the cast and to bring audience and actor too close together. Unless the audience sits at some distance from the stage, and at a higher sight line, a director will have great difficulty in establishing effective blocking for asides, mime, and dance. With stage right an exit to the forum and stage left an exit to the country (or the harbor, or the market), the actors need a long, shallow playing area for most scenes. As a general principle, the stage design should underscore visually the nonillusory nature of the plays: bright, primary colors for sets and costumes, exaggerated clown make-up for the actors' faces. (Masks should not be attempted, both because the present scripts are written for actors who use their faces, and because the authenticity of masks for Plautus remains an open question.) In sum, the way a production looks should complement the way the characters speak and act upon the stage.

The important principle to keep in mind is that Plautus must *not* be performed in a realistic style. The broader the style of acting, the better. He is closer to the Marx Brothers than to Molière. His plays have nothing whatever to do with psychological plausibility or the orderly development of a plot. His works are farces which must be played with no effort at creating a realistic illusion. Just as his language is self-conscious, and constantly calling our attention to that fact, so too the style of acting that he demands must be self-conscious, very much on the surface of things. His is a theater always conscious of its own theatrical nature, one which always reminds the audience that they are watching a play.[16] An aside such as this one from *Casina* requires the performer to deliver not only the lines but also a commentary on those lines:

LYSIDAMUS [*falls on his knees*]
But, wife, grant pardon to your husband.

[*Turns to Myrrhina*]

Myrrhina, plead with Cleostrata for me.

[To company and audience]

If I ever fall in love with Casina after this, or if I ever begin to—not to speak of making love—if I ever hereafter do anything of the sort

[To Cleostrata]

you'll have every right, my wife, to string me up by my thumbs and give me a sound lashing.

MYRRHINA *[eagerly]*:   Oh, I think *this* pardon ought to be granted!

CLEOSTRATA *[grimly]*:   I'll do as you say.

[Turns to audience, brightly]

And the main reason I shall grant this pardon now, and with less reluctance, is to avoid making a long play even longer than it already is.

One suggestion may be offered about the actual performance itself. Plautus is a calculating playwright who builds his comic effects by means of a surprisingly economical number of scenes. There should never be an intermission in the performance of Plautine comedy. The longest of these three plays is *Bacchides,* and it runs a little under two hours. To break the action at any point can easily destroy a comedy's dynamics. If the audience knows there will be no break, and if the director sets a properly fast pace to the action, crowding one scene on another, the comic energies inherent in Plautus's text will easily sustain the performance in a single continuum.

READING VERSUS PERFORMING PLAUTUS

The versions of *Bacchides, Casina,* and *Truculentus* in this volume are intended to serve primarily as scripts for the theater rather than as literary texts for silent reading. The critical perspective for this attitude to a dramatic text will be familiar to readers of Granville-Barker's *Prefaces* to the plays of Shakespeare; he respected Shakespeare's text, but he also insisted that that same printed text be envisioned as a means to the theatrical experience the playwright sought to create.[17] A play's script is designed to create an experience to be enacted in a theater, where the audience becomes as important a part of the dramatic experience as the actors themselves. Recent criticism has shown that this principle can apply as well to Aeschylus as it does to Shakespeare.[18]

If it is difficult to appreciate Plautus in a silent reading, even a group reading of a play will not accomplish everything. As the actors in *Casina* discovered when they performed the play without audience for a videotape recording, such a comedy is a verbal and visual farce which does not easily come to life unless there is an audience present.[19] Many scenes that worked brilliantly in performance before an audience became flat and lifeless in the empty theater. I hope that readers of these versions of *Bacchides, Casina,* and *Truculentus* will strive to keep that dimension of theater before them. The fairest judgment of Plautus will come from performance, or at least from a performance imagined in the mind of the reader. The stage directions show how a scene can be played, but of course the direction of any scene could go in quite different ways from what is outlined here.

USING THIS VOLUME

For the meanings and pronunciation of Greek or Latin words, the reader should consult the glossary and pronunciation guide at the end of this book. The line numbers of the original Latin will only occasionally be referred to in the notes. I have maintained the traditional divisions into acts and scenes solely for the sake of convenient reference to the text of the translations. The traditional division into acts and scenes is a procrustean invention of J. B. Pius for his edition of the comedies in 1500. Pius's aim was to make Plautus's comedy fit the famous "five-act rule" of Horace and other ancient authorities. He divided scenes by indicating a change with the entrance of any new actor, and divided acts by taking note of what were supposed to be major pauses in the action. This is exactly like the traditional five-act divisions of Shakespeare, and potentially just as misleading. As a glance at acts IV and V of *Bacchides* will show, such act divisions often do not reveal the true dramatic structure of a play.

NOTES

1. Only criticism available in English will be cited here. The standard handbook to consult is George E. Duckworth, *The Nature of Roman Comedy* (Princeton, 1952); see also W. Beare, *The Roman Stage*, 3d ed. (London, 1964). For comprehensive surveys of later Plautine scholarship see John A. Hanson, "Scholarship on Plautus since 1950," pts. 1 and 2, *The Classical World* 59 (1964): 101–29 and 60 (1966): 141–48; and Erich Segal, "Scholarship on Plautus since 1966," ibid., 74 (1981): 353–433. More detailed remarks about each of the plays can be found in the essays introducing each translation.

2. See Duckworth, *The Nature of Roman Comedy*, pp. 49–51, for a concise summary of the evidence.

3. For a readable and performable translation of Menander's only complete comedy see Carrol Moulton, *The Dyskolos of Menander* (New York, 1977).

4. For a sociological reading of a Plautine comedy see David Konstan, "Plautus' *Captivi* and the Ideology of the Ancient City State," *Ramus* 5 (1976): 76–91.

5. An excellent and sympathetic study of Menander's dramatic art is now available in Sander M. Goldberg, *The Making of Menander's Comedy* (Berkeley and Los Angeles, 1980).

6. For an analysis of possible parallels between Scipio the Elder and the characters Jupiter and Amphitryon see G. K. Galinsky, "Scipionic Themes in Plautus' *Amphitruo*," *Transactions and Proceedings of the American Philological Association* 97 (1966): 203–35. Typical of the delicacy of the relationship between poet and politician is the often cited transgression of Plautus's contemporary Naevius: A verse in one of his plays (*Fato Metelli Romae fiunt consules*, "By Fate the Metelli are made consuls of Rome") was ambiguous; *fato* could mean "by Fate" or "to the misfortune of Rome." Metellus (consul in 206 B.C.) was said to have replied, *Dabunt malum Metelli Naevio poetae*, "The Metelli will cause the poet Naevius a lot of trouble." Naevius was subsequently thrown into prison.

7. For an ancient account of the wars with Hannibal (and a good indication of how deep an impression those wars still made on the Roman psyche two centuries later) see Livy *A History of Rome* (*Ab Urbe Condita*), bks. 21–30; for a modern historian's account see H. H. Scullard, *A History of the Roman World from 753 to 146 B.C.*, 3d ed. (London, 1961), pp. 133–331.

8. For Plautine comedy's mockery of such Roman virtues as *gravitas* (seriousness of character) and *pietas* (sense of duty) see Erich Segal, *Roman Laughter* (Cambridge, Mass., 1968). Segal's theory owes much to C. L. Barber, *Shakespeare's Festive Comedy* (Princeton, 1959).

9. ". . . Plautus, whose work is among the most sombre in the world's literature, though that is not its reputation" (Simone Weil, "The Great Beast: Some Reflections on the Origins of Hitlerism," in *Selected Essays, 1934–1943*, selected and translated by Richard Rees [Oxford, London, and Toronto, 1962], p. 121).

10. Northrop Frye, *The Anatomy of Criticism* (Princeton, 1957), p. 167.

11. No translations of *Bacchides* and *Truculentus* have appeared since George E. Duckworth's *The Complete Roman Drama* (New York, 1942). Paul Nixon's translations from 1916 to 1938 in the Loeb edition are in fact more durable; see Paul Nixon, *Plautus*, 5 vols. (Cambridge, Mass., and London, 1979).

12. See Robert W. Corrigan, "Translating for Actors," in *The Craft and Context of Translation*, ed. William Arrowsmith and Roger Shattuck (Austin, 1961), pp. 95–106.

13. There is an astringent but helpful discussion of the subject in Beare, *Roman Stage*, pp. 219–32.

14. Consider the entrance of Cleostrata in act II of *Casina*. In a passage of some fifty lines, she and her confidant Myrrhina speak in over twenty different meters. To give an idea of the complexity, a partial list of the meters (− = long syllable, ∪ = short syllable) would include the anapaestic octonarius (∪∪− × 8), the cretic tetrameter (−∪− × 4), the anapaestic tetrameter (∪∪− × 4), iambic dimeter (∪− × 2), the bacchiac dimeter and tetrameter (∪− − × 2 and ∪− − × 4), the trochaic tetrameter (−∪ × 4), the choriambic dimeter (−∪∪− × 2), and the glyconic (−∪∪−∪∪). Such asymmetry in versification has no parallel in English prosody. To attempt to reproduce the meters of the *cantica* exactly line by line would yield something quite alien to our ears.

15. But for a recent investigation of the tradition of performance in Plautus's day see Bruno Gentili, *Theatrical Performances in the Ancient World: Hellenistic and Early Roman Theater* (Amsterdam, 1979).

16. This critical perspective, new to the study of Plautus, is brilliantly developed in Niall W. Slater's "The Theatre of the Mind: Metatheatre in Plautus" (Ph.D. diss., Princeton University, 1981).

17. Harley Granville-Barker, *Prefaces to Shakespeare* (Princeton, 1965).

18. See Michael Goldman, *Shakespeare and the Energies of Drama* (Princeton, 1972); and Oliver Taplin, *Greek Tragedy in Action* (Berkeley, Los Angeles, and London, 1979).

19. See J. L. Styan, *The Elements of Drama* (Cambridge, 1960), esp. pp. 231–55; and idem, *Drama, Stage, and Audience* (Cambridge, 1975), pp. 224–41.

BACCHIDES
or
TWO SISTERS NAMED BACCHIS

THE PRODUCERS

Bacchides has been esteemed more often for its parts than for its effectiveness in the theater. Through an unknown *florilegium* or medieval anthology of tags and quotable verses it inspired one of the most famous lines in European poetry: "Abandon every hope, you who enter here" (*Lasciate ogni speranza, voi ch' entrate*), the words written above the entrance to Hell in Dante's *Inferno*. The idea of the abandonment of hope at the entrance to the underworld first appeared as a metaphor in a monologue of one of the characters in act III, scene 1, of *Bacchides*, in a very different setting. The tutor Lydus is seeking to flee, not the gateway to the pagan underworld, but the doorway of a whorehouse.[1]

> Ope' wide at once this door to Hades!
> I beg you, unlock the door!
> Yes, a door to Hades and nothing less:
> no one comes this way unless he has
> abandoned all hope who enters here.

Bacchides has more recently attracted readers for what it reveals about Plautus's use of Greek sources and his originality in adapting Greek New Comedy to the Roman stage. The play had long been known to be based on Menander's lost comedy *The Double Deceiver* (*Dis Exapaton*). The discovery and publication of an extensive papyrus fragment from that play in 1968 made it possible to compare a sequence of seventy lines in Plautus (*Bacchides* III.3–III.6) with the original scene in Menander.[2] Comparison shows that Plautus is an exact or free translator, depending on his own dramatic purposes. He aimed of course to write a play quite different from the naturalistic comedy of Menander.[3] Efforts to reconstruct the lost opening scene have contributed a great deal to our understanding of the play, since a clear sense of the entire comedy is required if one is to write a performable and dramatically coherent opening.[4] But no script can be seen in clear outline, nor its theatricality easily assessed, until it is produced; and in performance *Bacchides* at once comes into focus as a peculiar play. It appears to be willfully eccentric in its dramatic structure, with a concluding scene which seems at first sight to be gratuitously cynical, almost an afterthought to the main action.

Bacchides could be summed up as a play about two young men willing to do anything for love who are passionately devoted to two courtesans who will do anything for money. Thanks to the machinations of a clever slave, both pairs get what they want. The audience gets a good deal more. *Bacchides* seems to have two of everything. Besides the sisters Bacchis (Bacchis of Athens and her sister Bacchis visiting from Samos, here named Bacchis I and Bacchis II) and their young men (Pistoclerus and Mnesilochus), there are the two fathers (Philoxenus and Nicobulus) and two slaves (the tutor Lydus and the mastermind Chrysalus). There also seem to be two plays. The two sisters Bacchis who give their name to *Bacchides* are peripheral to most of its action; they appear only in the opening and closing scenes. For nearly a thousand lines and all but twenty minutes of performance time, the stage is given to the slave Chrysalus and his ingenious plots to unite the young men with the sisters Bacchis. A more detailed summary is needed to appreciate the particular logic of this play, for it does have a logic that works in the theater.

Bacchis I learns that her sister has returned to Athens, but under contract for one year to the soldier Cleomachus. To free her from this obligation, the two sisters call on young Pistoclerus. Since Pistoclerus's best friend, Mnesilochus, is in love with Bacchis II, Pistoclerus can do a double favor to his mistress and his friend. The sisters then retire. Pistoclerus first turns aside the warnings of his tutor Lydus about the evils of the Bacchis sisters, then commissions the slave Chrysalus to take care of the matter. Chrysalus does this by persuading the old man Nicobulus that the money he had entrusted to Chrysalus and his son Mnesilochus was stolen by a perfidious Greek at Ephesus named Archidemides. The entire sum is in fact untouched and under the guard of Mnesilochus. Chrysalus's scheme works perfectly until Mnesilochus arrives. Overhearing a long harangue by Lydus about Pistoclerus's affair with Bacchis I, he assumes that his best friend has betrayed him and stolen Bacchis II. In a fit of jealousy, Mnesilochus turns over all the money he was bringing from Ephesus. Chrysalus's plot is now exposed to Nicobulus.

Mnesilochus and Pistoclerus are soon reconciled and turn quickly to Chrysalus for another plot. This time his trick consists in appearing to offer sound advice and good evidence. By dictating several letters to Mnesilochus, Chrysalus successfully portrays himself as an injured innocent who is trying to save Nicobulus and his son from the boy's own foolishness. When the soldier, Cleomachus suddenly appears, Chrysalus outdoes himself by persuading Nicobulus that Bacchis I is the *wife* of Cleomachus. Terrified for his son's safety, the old man guarantees repayment of Bacchis II's fee. Once Chrysalus has won his second game of deception, he celebrates his triumph, walks off the stage and out of the play. Nicobulus discovers the truth too late, since he has paid the fee twice, once to his son and once to the soldier. He is joined by Philoxenus. Both old men charge in a rage to Bacchis I's door and summon the sisters outdoors. After a quick consultation, Bacchis I and Bacchis II decide to lure the old men inside so that their sons' expenses can be kept up. Philoxenus easily gives in, and after increasingly weaker protests, so does Nicobulus. Fathers and sons end the day in the same bed, with the two sisters named Bacchis.

Bacchis I and Bacchis II run an elaborate establishment which they support through the systematic seduction of their customers.[5] These men think of themselves as lovers (*amantes*), but in the eye of Bacchis I and II they are merely sources of income.[6] In *Bacchides* the usual business of the courtesans, seduction, is supplemented by another way of making money: the elaborately staged production of Chrysalus's double deception, and a production in no figurative sense. Producers supervise the performance of a play, and they profit from it, but they do not direct it or act in it. This is precisely what Bacchis I and II do. They seduce Pistoclerus, then commission him to get money, and he in turn commissions Chrysalus to contrive a plot. Although he is willing to play any role necessary, Pistoclerus is like any actor in that he himself has no idea what that role may be. Chrysalus is more obliging.

Bacchides is thus the property of its producers, the sisters Bacchis. They are the only players comparable to Chrysalus. Where he uses his wit to manipulate others, they use their beauty; and his wit is itself in service to that beauty. Every other character in the play is only a person to be manipulated. Although Lydus at first seems to be a vivid exception to the rule, he is finally ordered into obedience by his masters. His moralizing convinces no one, least of all Pistoclerus, who appears to have learned only rhetoric from his teacher, not good sense. While Nicobulus may seem to be made of sterner stuff and to have produced a better son, Mnesilochus is distinguished mainly for his narcissistic soliloquies. Like theatrical producers in real life, Bacchis I and her sister are able to withdraw from most of the turmoil of the drama which the director Chrysalus creates.

Chrysalus will remind many readers of Pseudolus, the clever slave turned playwright in the later comedy *Pseudolus,* produced in 191 B.C.[7] Without the misapprehension of Mnesilochus, Chrysalus's first deception would have worked. His task was to invent a believable fiction. He fails because he is not at first fully in charge of the stage he attempts to control. Mnesilochus's indiscretion undoes everything, and because of the unreliable forces he works with, Chrysalus must move from a plot of innocent mariners threatened by pirates and swindled by Greeks to a plot characterized by an imagery of warfare. And war it is, since his task is far more difficult the second time around; his victim knows about the first plot and is on guard against further tricks. Hence Chrysalus becomes "General Chrysalus," *imperator Chrysalus* (IV.4):

CHRYSALUS
> Now, pay attention, Mnesilochus, and you too,
> Pistoclerus.
> Both of you go now into the dining room.
> Take your places on that twin-sized couch of yours.
> Once you're set up there, your job is to start drinking.
> That's an order.
> PISTOCLERUS: Any more orders?
> CHRYSALUS: One more: once you've taken your places,
> don't dare leave unless you get a signal from me.
> PISTOCLERUS: Oh noble general!

When Chrysalus no longer needs his not too competent soldiers, he orders them off the stage and out of the play. The imagery of an army on the march culminates in the showpiece of *Bacchides*, the Song of Troy (IV.9). Nicobulus is likened to Priam and besieged Troy, and Chrysalus is cast as the Greeks—Ulysses, Agamemnon, Menelaus, Ajax, and Achilles rolled into one. Like a Roman general leading his troops home, he offers a report of his conquests, modestly declines the honor of a triumph, and leaves the stage (IV.9).

Although Chrysalus congratulates himself on a well-run campaign, he in fact leaves behind some unfinished business which only the Bacchis sisters can complete. An audience may wonder why the sisters need to reappear. There are no threads left to tie up from the opening scene. Neither Mnesilochus nor Pistoclerus is a serious romantic interest for Bacchis I or II. Recall then that money, not love, is essential to the courtesan; Nicobulus and Philoxenus unwittingly offer the sisters an unexpected source of further income. Nicobulus has paid twice, but he has not paid enough. He has also been tricked twice, but not enough. He has only discovered Chrysalus's plotting and trickery, but he and we have yet to discover what he really is. For all his indignation, he is a father not one bit better than his son. The epilogue spoken by the company is prim and to the point.

> If these two old men had not been worthless
> since boyhood, they'd not be snared in scandals
> today in their hoary manhood; nor would we
> much delight in our play's long survival,
> had we not often seen whores made rich
> by greedy sons and fathers playing rivals.

The joke on Nicobulus is not only that he was tricked twice and paid twice but that he thought he was a better man than other men, and was not. For him, this is costly knowledge. Thus *Bacchides* is a traditional comedy of deception, and more. Although we revel in Chrysalus's plots, we realize at the same time that his brilliant imagination serves other ends than our entertainment. While we have had a good time, two sisters named Bacchis have made a good deal of money. This is a complex message to leave with an audience.

BACCHIDES
or
TWO SISTERS
NAMED BACCHIS

CHARACTERS

RUNNING SLAVE, *servant of Bacchis I*
BACCHIS I, *courtesan of Athens*
BOY, *in service to Cleomachus*
BACCHIS II, *sister of Bacchis I, a courtesan arriving from Samos*
PISTOCLERUS, *young man of Athens, in love with Bacchis I*
LYDUS, *pedagogue, slave of Philoxenus and teacher of Pistoclerus*
CHRYSALUS, *slave of Mnesilochus and Nicobulus*
NICOBULUS, *old man of Athens*
MNESILOCHUS, *son of Nicobulus*
PHILOXENUS, *old man of Athens, father of Pistoclerus*
PARASITE, *in service to Cleomachus*
ARTAMO, *slave overseer of Nicobulus*
CLEOMACHUS, *soldier*

[*Scene:* A street in Athens with the houses of Bacchis I and Nicobulus]

I.1.A[1]
[*Running Slave runs on to stage; darts back and forth, finally comes to Bacchis I's door; bangs loudly*]

RUNNING SLAVE: She's here! She's here! Is anybody home?
BACCHIS I [*inside*]: Who is here?

[*Comes out*]

RUNNING SLAVE: Bacchis is here.

BACCHIS I: You mean my sister?

RUNNING SLAVE: Yes, your sister.

BACCHIS I: My dear sister Bacchis from Samos?

RUNNING SLAVE: Yes, Bacchis from Samos.

BACCHIS I: The one who is as much like me as one drop of milk is like another?

RUNNING SLAVE: Yes, it's her.

BACCHIS I: The sister who has the same name as mine?

RUNNING SLAVE: The very same one.

BACCHIS I [sends Running Slave into house]:   All right, inside at once! Out with the pails and water! Bring on the brooms! I want this house in order for the arrival of my dear, dear sister.

[Running Slave dashes inside. Servants start running around, cleaning, dusting, etc. Bacchis I confides to audience]

Bless her heart. She's been living in Ephesus and sent me a letter saying that she had snared a rich young man from Athens. In fact, he's the son of my next-door neighbor Nicobulus. [Gestures towards Nicobulus's house, next-door] But then she found an even bigger catch: a stupid mercenary soldier. You know, the kind that sells his life for gold. Too bad for the boy next-door, but business is business. She says the soldier is all boasting and bellowing. The only reason she agreed to go with him was that he offered to pay her a huge salary for one whole year. [Laughs] What it must be like to be in his service! All huffing and puffing! Banging in bed with him must be noisier than the banging in a blacksmith's shop.

BOY [enters leading train with Bacchis II and slaves carrying her baggage]:   Which house is it, you say?

BACCHIS II: Why, this house. Wouldn't I know the house of my own sister? In fact, there she is, standing at the door! Oh, sister dear! Greetings! Here I am, back in dear old Athens again.

BACCHIS I: Greetings! Is it really you? Home after all this time?

BACCHIS II: Yes, home after a whole year abroad.

[They embrace warmly]

BOY [unimpressed, to audience]:   Abroad? Why are they so excited about being abroad?

BACCHIS I: I am so delighted at the news of the soldier, dear. I only regret you had to give up my neighbor's boy Mnesilochus to get him.

BACCHIS II: Yes, even though he doesn't have much money, his father does, and that's what really counts.

BACCHIS I: Indeed it does. If only there were some way to keep you here in Athens for a year. You would earn *far* more from Nicobulus and his son if you did.

BOY [*breaks in indignantly, to Bacchis II*]: What plot are you two plotting? Don't you know you're hired out to my master for a year? You're not supposed to take a fee from any man but him for one whole year! And no belly-bumping with anybody else, either.

BACCHIS II [*chases him away*]: Shut up, you little slug! Go back to the harbor this instant! You're supposed to wait there until your master arrives. When he does, bring him here to my sister's house.

BOY [*slinks away, muttering to audience*]: What good does it do to be a loyal slave? Curses if you're honest, the whip and the whipping post if you're not.

[*Exit*]

BACCHIS I: I wish there were some way we could keep you here, sister dear. There's so much money in my neighbor's house.

[*Enter Pistoclerus. He does not at first notice the two sisters standing in front of Bacchis's house*]

PISTOCLERUS [*to audience, holding up a letter*]
Just today I received a letter from my old pal Mnesilochus.
He's the son of Nicobulus, the old man who lives here.
He's been away in Ephesus on business for his father.
He says that he's fallen in love with a woman from Samos,
a woman named Bacchis, and *that's* quite a coincidence,
because I happen to be in love with her sister Bacchis,
the one from Athens. He asks me to do anything I can
to free *his* Bacchis from some soldier named Cleomachus.
He says this Cleomachus has hired her for a whole year
and that this soldier Cleomachus is bringing her to Athens.
He wants me to get *his* Bacchis away from the soldier,
one way or another. I don't have any idea

how I'll do all that, but I know one thing
for sure: I'd do anything for my old pal.[2]

BACCHIS I [to Bacchis II]:   Look, dear! It's my latest catch, Pistoclerus,
the son of that rich old man Philoxenus! He's the one that will
save us.

PISTOCLERUS [catching sight of Bacchis I and Bacchis II; to audi-
ence]:   Why, what's this I see? It's my very own mistress,
Bacchis, and her sister . . . Bacchis . . . the one who has my old
pal all aflame. I'd do anything in the world for her . . . for
Bacchis . . . my Bacchis, that is . . . not her sister Bacchis. [Runs
over] My honeybuns! My heart! My hope! My sweetie! My
food! My joy!

[Kneels, embraces Bacchis I around the waist]

BACCHIS I: Pistoclerus! Dear, dear Pistoclerus, how sweet you are!

[Signals to Bacchis II to step over to one side]

BACCHIS II [steps to one side; to audience]:   Ah! So this is the young man
my sister has been working on! While his friend Mnesilochus
was off on business with me in Ephesus, he stayed behind in
Athens. If you ask me, he's strayed as far from home as his
friend. They say that Ulysses had a terrible time wandering
away from home for twenty years. But Pistoclerus has outdone him, and all his wanderings have taken place right
inside the walls of Athens!

PISTOCLERUS [to Bacchis I]:   Honeybuns, you could charm the heart
of any man you pleased.

BACCHIS I [peels off each hand, fastidiously]:   Yes, dear, I know. Now let
me have a word with my sister. [Crosses to Bacchis II] Sister,
dear, do you see what I see?

BACCHIS II [surveying goggle-eyed Pistoclerus with a professional
eye]:   H'm . . . why, yes, dear sister, I think I do. He's the
fellow who will get me out of that contract with the soldier
and into the house of Mnesilochus and his father Nicobulus.

BACCHIS I: You're right, dear. And aren't you relieved we have
Plautus now to help us play this play?

BACCHIS II [with relief]:   Oh dear, yes! He's been kept out of it too
long as it is!

I.1.B

BACCHIS I [*to Bacchis II*]:   Just keep quiet and let *me* do most of the talking.

BACCHIS II: Fine, go ahead.

BACCHIS I: If my memory fails me, do come to my aid, sister dear.

BACCHIS II: Dear sister, *me* sing *your* tune? I know I'll fail.[3]

BACCHIS I: Why, sister dear, you, our bedroom nightingale?

[*They go over to Pistoclerus*]

PISTOCLERUS [*aside*]:   What are those twin sisters with one name up to? [*To Bacchis I and Bacchis II*] What schemes have you been scheming?

BACCHIS I: Nice ones.

PISTOCLERUS [*aside*]:   I see. [*To Bacchis I*] Not at all in your usual style.

BACCHIS I [*attempts the tragic style*]:   Who is there more miserable than a woman?

PISTOCLERUS: Who would you say more deserves to be?

BACCHIS I: My sister here wants me to find some man to protect her, so that the soldier—[*Bacchis II signals worriedly to her, she catches herself*] I mean that man can take her home when her rental time is up. [*Leaning on him*] Would you please look after her?

PISTOCLERUS: Look after her? how? [*Again on his knees with arms around her*]

BACCHIS I [*again breaks the embrace; Pistoclerus falls to floor*]:   By taking her home when she's finished her job. Then the soldier won't have her for his housemaid. You see, if he got back the money he paid for her, he'd be glad to let her go.

PISTOCLERUS [*on all fours*]:   Where is he now?

BACCHIS I: I think he'll arrive at any moment. But it would be better for you to come to our house. You can sit there and wait until he comes. You'll have wine, and I'll give you a kiss with your drink.

PISTOCLERUS [*arising*]:   Your sweet words are pure birdlime.

BACCHIS I: What do you mean?

PISTOCLERUS [*striking a pose*]:   Because I know that two of you are after one pigeon. [*Bacchis I and Bacchis II each take him by one arm*] Damn! [*Aside*] Those birdlime twigs are brushing my wings! [*He breaks free*] Look, you, I don't see any profit for me in this crime.

BACCHIS I: Why, dear?

PISTOCLERUS: Why? Because I'm afraid of you bacchantes and your bacchanals, Bacchis.

BACCHIS I: What is it? What are you afraid of? You don't mean my *bed* is tempting you to do something naughty?

PISTOCLERUS: I'm more afraid of your *head* than your bed. [*Aside*] You're a wicked beast! [*Resumes*] Look, you, your dank, dark den is no profitable place for a young fellow like me.

BACCHIS I: You know I would stop you myself if you tried to do anything foolish at my house. [*He grabs for her again; she glides away and shifts to a businesslike tone*] Now, when the soldier comes, I want you to be at my house; that way no one will do her or me any harm, not as long as you're around. You'll help us, and the help you give us will help your *old pal*. When he comes, he'll think I'm your girl friend. [*Pistoclerus is already baffled by all this*] Now, dear, why are you so quiet?

PISTOCLERUS [*strikes a moral pose*]

Your words are charming to listen to,
but test them and you'll find their thorns:
they pierce the heart, they squander fortunes,
they wound us and our reputation.

BACCHIS II [*interposes*]: Why are you afraid of her?

PISTOCLERUS

Why am I afraid of her?
Should a young man like me go into a gymnasium like *this*,
to sweat away his wealth into bankruptcy? [*Warming to his theme*] Where I'd take on a DEBT instead of a DISCUS? RUINATION instead of RUNNING?

BACCHIS I [*both sisters are resigned to this fit of eloquence*]: Oh, how charming!

PISTOCLERUS [*striding about*]

Where I'd take up "MY TURTLE DOVE" instead of my SWORD?
A GOBLET instead of a HELMET?
A GARLAND instead of a STANDARD?
DICE instead of a SPEAR?
SISSY GREEK GARMENTS
instead of the REINS OF A STALWART STEED?
RIDE A LOVER'S COUCH INSTEAD OF A HORSE?

STRAP ON A BROAD INSTEAD OF A BUCKLER?
OH NO! NOT ME!

[*In a frenzy*]

AWAY WITH YOU! AWAY I SAY!

[*Recovering himself, he stares nobly into the distance*]

BACCHIS I [*caressing him*]:   Oh, you're much too hard on us.

PISTOCLERUS [*responding to her hands*]:   Not nearly as hard as I am on myself.

BACCHIS I [*fondles him*]:   I'll have to take you in hand myself. You need to *relax.*

PISTOCLERUS [*draws back in shock*]:   Ah, your handcraft costs too much.

BACCHIS I: Then make believe you're in love with me!

PISTOCLERUS [*falls on his knees again, embracing her*]:   Should I make believe for a joke or play like I mean business?

BACCHIS I: NOT NOW! [*peels him off and straightens her clothing; in businesslike tone again*] This is what I want to do: when the soldier arrives, I want you to hug me.

PISTOCLERUS [*still on his knees*]:   Why should I do that?

BACCHIS I [*exasperated at his slowness*]:   I want him to see you. [*Interrupts his protest*] I know what I'm doing.

PISTOCLERUS: God knows, I'm afraid you do. But look here...

BACCHIS I: Yes?

PISTOCLERUS: What if all of a sudden you happened to have a lunch, or a round of drinks, or a dinner? You know, the sort of thing that usually happens at little get-togethers like yours? Where would I be then?

BACCHIS I: Next to me, my heart and soul: a nice boy and a nice girl, side by side. You'll always have a free place at our house, no matter how unexpectedly you show up. Whenever you need to have a nice time, just say to me, [*She bends him over in an embrace; in rasping baritone*] "Hey, Rosie...you got a nice place for me?" [*She kisses him, then drops him to the floor; surveying his prostrate form*] I'll be sure to give you a *nice place* to rest in.

PISTOCLERUS [*aside, from the floor*]:   This is one rapid river! No quick and easy crossing here!

BACCHIS I [*aside*]:   And it's a river you're likely to lose something in, too. [*Abruptly*] Now, give me your hand and follow me.

PISTOCLERUS: Oh no! Absolutely not!

BACCHIS I: Why not?

PISTOCLERUS [*still on the floor*]:   Because there could be no combination more tempting than this: a night, a woman, wine, and a *young innocent* like me.

[*He stares dewy-eyed into the distance*]

BACCHIS I [*revolted at this narcissism, she feigns resignation*]:   Very well! I don't mind at all. Anything for you, dear. Let the soldier take her away. You don't have to be there if you don't want to.

PISTOCLERUS [*aside, still on the floor*]:   So I'm worthless, eh? Got no will power at all, eh?

BACCHIS I: What are you afraid of?

PISTOCLERUS [*crawls over to her*]:   Nothing, dear. A mere trifle. I surrender, dear. I am yours. I am at your service.

[*Clasps her around the middle*]

BACCHIS I [*with a triumphant glance to her sister*]:   What a nice boy! [*Again peels his hand away and resumes her businesslike tone; Pistoclerus watches her with gaping mouth*] Now, this is what I want you to do. I want to give a homecoming dinner for my sister. I'll order the servants inside to bring you some money. Then you go and get us the most gorgeous groceries you can find.

PISTOCLERUS: No, I'll pay for the groceries myself! It would be to my everlasting shame to have you, a mere woman, work for me and pay all the bills as well.

BACCHIS I: But I don't want a single thing from you!

[*Bacchis II turns away giggling*]

PISTOCLERUS: Oh, do let me!

BACCHIS I [*feigns great reluctance*]:   Well. . .if you want to. . .all right. [*Pistoclerus starts to kiss her; she pushes him off*] Please, do hurry along.

PISTOCLERUS [*starts to go; turns, with outstretched arms*]:   I'll be back long before my love for you cools off.

[*Exits backward to forum, with arms outstretched*]

BACCHIS II [*collapses in laughter*]:   You've prepared a splendid enter-
tainment for my arrival, my darling sister!
BACCHIS I: Indeed, why do you think so?
BACCHIS II: You've netted quite a little catch in your net, as I see it.
BACCHIS I: Yes, he is a nice catch. Now I'll have to help you with
Mnesilochus, sister dear. You can make your money here
instead of having to go off with the soldier.
BACCHIS II: Exactly what I want.
BACCHIS I [*advances to house*]:   To work! The water's hot. Let's go
inside so you can take a bath. I imagine the ups and downs of
a sea voyage left you a little shaky for this kind of work?
BACCHIS II: Possibly a little, dear sister. Let's go now. [*Sounds of the
approach of Lydus, Pistoclerus, and their train*] Listen! Someone is
coming.
BACCHIS I: Follow me in, then. You need to relax after your
journey.

[*Exeunt*]

I.2
[*Enter Pistoclerus with attendants carrying provisions, wine, flowers. He is
followed by his teacher Lydus*]
LYDUS [*in fussy manner*]:   Now, Pistoclerus, I've been following you
silently for some time to see what you're going to do with all
this. [*Gestures towards provisions*] May the gods bless me! I think
even a senator would be tempted to naughtiness here![4]
Where are you going with so much fancy food?
PISTOCLERUS: Here.

[*Points to the house of Bacchis I*]

LYDUS: Here? What do you mean "here"? Who lives there?
PISTOCLERUS [*in ecstasy*]
Who? Oh, Love, Pleasure, Venus, Grace, Joy,
Jest, Sport, Chatter, Smoochabella.[5]

[*Smacks lips*]

LYDUS [*shocked*]:   What business have you with such god-awful
gods?
PISTOCLERUS [*strikes moral pose*]

"Evil is that man who of good men does evil say."[6]
You're not addressing these gods properly.

[*Wagging finger*]

That's *wrong*.

LYDUS: You mean to say there is a god named Smoochabella?

[*Smacking lips*]

PISTOCLERUS
You mean to say you thought there wasn't?
You really *are* a barbarian Lydian, Lydus.[7]
You, the man I once thought knew more than Thales,
why, you know less than a baby barbarian!
At your age! Not knowing the names of the gods!

LYDUS [*gesturing towards provisions*]:   I don't like the looks of this.

PISTOCLERUS: Well, no one brought it here for you. It was brought here for me, and I do like it.

LYDUS: So *now* you're starting to use smart talk with me? You, who ought to keep silent even if you had ten tongues?

PISTOCLERUS: You can't play the lead in every game in life, Lydus. What I'm most concerned with now is whether the cook's concoctions will do justice to this food.

LYDUS
Now you've wasted yourself and me and my good works—
me, who so often advised you so well. All, all in vain!

[*Raises arm to brow in tragic style*]

PISTOCLERUS [*unimpressed*]:   I wasted my "good works" the same place you wasted yours. Your brand of education was of no use to me or you.

LYDUS [*in tragic style*]:   Oh what a heart hardened to hardness!

PISTOCLERUS: Oh what a bore! Keep quiet and follow me, Lydus.

LYDUS [*to audience*]:   Just listen to that! He doesn't call me "teacher" now, just "Lydus"!

PISTOCLERUS: It wouldn't be right or proper to have "teacher" along when a man has gone to all the trouble of buying so much food, and is lying on his mistress's couch—especially not with all those other guests around, too.

LYDUS [*shocked again*]:   Good heavens! You mean you brought provisions here for *that* kind of party?

PISTOCLERUS [*again strikes moral pose*]

"The heart hath hopes; their outcome lies

, in the hands of god alone."

LYDUS: So you're determined to have a mistress, then?

PISTOCLERUS: When you see her you'll get the answer to that question.

[*Goes to Bacchis I's door*]

LYDUS [*blocking his way*]: Oh no you don't! You'll not have her, nor will I allow it! You go home this minute!

PISTOCLERUS: Just drop it, Lydus. Save yourself the trouble.

LYDUS: What do you mean, "Save yourself the trouble"?

PISTOCLERUS: I'm long past the age where I need your consent.

LYDUS [*in supertragic style, to the audience*]

Oh, infernal pit, where art thou now?

How gladly would I come to thee!

I have seen more here than I could have wished.

It were a far, far better thing to have died

than to have lived to see this.

That a pupil should so threaten his teacher!

[*Crumples dramatically to the floor*]

PISTOCLERUS [*stepping over him; straddling him*]

I think I'll play the role of Hercules.

You know, he *killed* his teacher Linus.[8]

LYDUS [*jumps up*]

And I'm afraid *I*'ll have to play the teacher Phoenix

and tell your father of the death of his little Achilles!

PISTOCLERUS [*dryly*]

That's enough Greek mythology for now, Lydus.

[*Starts again for door of Bacchis I's house*]

LYDUS [*to audience*]: He's beyond all shame. [*Goes to block door; to Pistoclerus*] This show of insolence is no credit to your years. [*To audience*] I'm destroyed. [*To Pistoclerus*] Have you forgotten that you have a father?

PISTOCLERUS: Who's the slave here—you or me?

LYDUS

Some wicked teacher taught you these ways, not me.

I see you're more teachable in these subjects

than in the ones I wasted my time trying to teach you.
That you could commit such crimes at your age!
That you could conceal them from me and your father!

PISTOCLERUS [*silences him with a wave*]: You've had enough free
speech for now, Lydus. Just follow me in and keep quiet.

[*They enter the house of Bacchis I*]

II.1
[*Enter Chrysalus solo*]

CHRYSALUS
Land of my master, hail! Two years ago I left you
for Ephesus, and now I gladly see you once again.

[*Turns to altar to Apollo*]

I salute you, Apollo, you who dwell neighbor to our house.
I pray, don't let my master Nicobulus see me
before I meet his son Mnesilochus's old pal Pistoclerus.

[*To audience*]

You see, Mnesilochus sent him a letter about his mistress
Bacchis.

II.2
[*Enter Pistoclerus from the house of Bacchis I*]

PISTOCLERUS [*pushed onstage, he talks through door to Bacchis I*]: It's
odd that you keep nagging me to go so much when I couldn't
leave you even if I wanted to. [*To audience, with a sigh*] Fixed
and fettered by love, that's me.

CHRYSALUS [*rises*]: By the immortal gods, it's Pistoclerus! Oh Pistoclerus, greetings!

PISTOCLERUS: Why, greetings, Chrysalus.

CHRYSALUS [*Pistoclerus starts to talk; Chrysalus stops him*]: I'm going to
save you the trouble of making a speech. You are delighted
that I'm here, and I believe you. [*Pistoclerus tries to speak again;
Chrysalus stops him again*] You promise me entertainment and
a meal, as is only proper for someone returning from abroad.
[*Pistoclerus tries to interrupt again*] Why, how kind! I accept
your invitation. [*And again*] Oh yes, very best wishes to you

from your old pal. [*Yet again*] Then you ask, "How is he doing?" He's alive.

PISTOCLERUS: Is he really doing well?

CHRYSALUS: That's exactly what I wanted to find out from you.

PISTOCLERUS: How could I know that?

CHRYSALUS: Who would know better?

PISTOCLERUS: Well, how *do* I know?

CHRYSALUS: Here's how. If the woman he loves has been found, he's alive and well. If she hasn't been found, he's not so well, he's about to die. If she is here, then his money is lost and he's worthless anyway. [*Pistoclerus gapes in wonder at all this*] But what have you done about the instructions he sent you?

PISTOCLERUS: Do you think I'm the kind of man who would let him arrive without having done what his messenger told me to do? I'd rather live in Hades than do that.

CHRYSALUS: Then you have found Bacchis?

PISTOCLERUS: Yes, the one from Samos.

CHRYSALUS: Please be careful that no one handles her carelessly! You know how fragile Samian pottery is.

[*Guffaws*]

PISTOCLERUS: You're as witty as ever, I see.

CHRYSALUS: Now, please tell me where she is.

PISTOCLERUS: Here, in the house you just saw me come from.

CHRYSALUS [*to audience*]:   Now that *is* good news! She lives right next-door to us. [*To Pistoclerus*] Does she still remember Mnesilochus?

PISTOCLERUS: Does she still remember him? Why, she considers him her one and only man in the world.

CHRYSALUS: Amazing!

PISTOCLERUS: Why, you do believe her, don't you? And you know what else? The poor girl is pining away for love.

CHRYSALUS: That's nice to know.

PISTOCLERUS: And you know what else, Chrysalus? She doesn't let even one teeny-tiny moment pass by without saying his name.

CHRYSALUS: So much the better for her.

PISTOCLERUS: And you know what else?

CHRYSALUS: What else I know is that I'd rather be anywhere but here.

PISTOCLERUS: You don't object to hearing about your master's good fortune, do you?

CHRYSALUS [aside, to audience]: It's not his good fortune that makes me sick! It's your bad acting! I can't even watch a comedy by Plautus when an actor like you is acting in it. And that's one playwright I love as much as I love myself.[9] [To Pistoclerus] So you think Bacchis really is a good girl, eh?

PISTOCLERUS: Of course she is. If I didn't already have Venus herself, she would be *my* Juno.

CHRYSALUS [aside]: Well, now, Mnesilochus, it looks to me as if you have already got the woman you love. Now you need to find out how to pay for her. [Turns back to Pistoclerus] Perhaps you need gold?

PISTOCLERUS: Yes! As many gold coins as we can get.

CHRYSALUS: And perhaps you need them now?

PISTOCLERUS: In fact we need them sooner than that. The soldier is due any minute.

CHRYSALUS: Oh? there's a soldier too?

PISTOCLERUS: And he'll want gold for releasing Bacchis from her contract.

CHRYSALUS: Let him come when he pleases. But he had better not keep me waiting: there's plenty of gold at home. I'm not afraid of any man. I don't have to beg for anything as long as I can come up with a good lie. But you go inside now. I'll look after things here. Once you're there, tell Bacchis that Mnesilochus will be here any minute.

PISTOCLERUS: Just as you say.

[Exit]

CHRYSALUS [solo]: I am in charge of this gold business. We've brought twelve hundred solid gold coins from Ephesus which a friend there owed to the old man. Now to fabricate some fabrications to get that gold for my love-struck master. Uh-oh, our door is opening! Who's coming outside now?

II.3

[Nicobulus enters from his house]

NICOBULUS: I'll go down to the Piraeus to see if any merchant ships have come into port from Ephesus. I'm worried that my son has stayed there so long and has not come home yet.

CHRYSALUS [aside]:   Now, if only the gods will let me, I'll fleece him neatly! This is not time to go to sleep on the job. I'll make a Croesus out of Chrysalus.[10] Now for the ram and its golden fleece. I'll shear the gold right down to the roots! [Goes up to Nicobulus and salutes him formally] From slave Chrysalus to master Nicobulus: greetings!

NICOBULUS: Chrysalus! By the immortal gods, where is my son?

CHRYSALUS [miffed]:   Well, you could have at least returned my greetings first.

NICOBULUS [impatiently]:   Well, greetings. But where is Mnesilochus?

CHRYSALUS: He's alive, he's well.

NICOBULUS: Has he arrived?

CHRYSALUS: He has.

NICOBULUS: Thank the gods. I can breathe again! Is he still in good health?

CHRYSALUS: In Marathonically—no, Olympically—good health.

NICOBULUS: Now, then, what about the job I sent him to do in Ephesus? Did he get my money back from our friend Archidemides?

CHRYSALUS [wringing hands]:   Oh, woe! Nicobulus, my head and heart just split in two at the very mention of that person's name. Don't you realize that the man you call a friend is really a fiend?[11]

NICOBULUS: What do you mean?

CHRYSALUS: I'm sure that none of the four gods Moon, Sun, Daylight, or Fire ever shone on a more wicked man than he!

NICOBULUS: No man more wicked than Archidemides?

CHRYSALUS: That's what I said: than Archidemides.

NICOBULUS: What has he done?

CHRYSALUS: What hasn't he done? Why don't you ask me that? First of all, he began to lie to your son and denied that he owed you so much as one coin. [Nicobulus tries to interrupt; Chrysalus silences him] Then Mnesilochus at once called for your tried and true friend, the old man Pelagon. In his presence he showed him the token you gave your son to carry to him.

NICOBULUS: What happened when he showed him the token?

CHRYSALUS: He said it was a counterfeit and not his token at all. And what slanderous things he said to your innocent boy! He said that he had counterfeited other things too.

NICOBULUS: Well, did you get the money? I want to know!

CHRYSALUS: Oh yes, after the law courts rendered a verdict against him, he was convicted and paid out a fine of...let me see...twelve hundred gold coins.

NICOBULUS: That's exactly what he owed!

CHRYSALUS: But there's more. Listen. He wanted to give us a fight.

NICOBULUS: There's more?

CHRYSALUS [aside]: Now to swoop down for the kill.

NICOBULUS [raging, to audience]: I've been tricked! I entrusted my money to a bigger thief than all the Greeks who plundered Troy![12]

CHRYSALUS: Will you please listen?

NICOBULUS: Obviously I never knew what a greedy character he was.

CHRYSALUS: After we went off with our gold, we boarded ship and eagerly set sail for home. By chance, while I was sitting up on the deck, I happened to look around and I saw a long, mean-looking galley being readied to sail.

NICOBULUS: Oh no! I'm done for! That galley will ram my side!

CHRYSALUS: Your friend was part-owner of the ship, along with...uh...pirates!

NICOBULUS: How could I have been such an idiot as to trust him? His very name makes it clear that he would rob me. Archidemides—just like a *Greek*!

CHRYSALUS: This galley pulled off hoping to ambush our ship. I made sure to keep a watch to see what they were up to. In the meantime our own ship set sail from the harbor. Once we were out of port, they began rowing after us. Neither birds nor winds could have been faster. When that happened, we stopped our ship at once. When they saw us stop they began to slow down their own ship in the harbor.

NICOBULUS: Oh gods, what devils they are! What did you do then?

CHRYSALUS: We went back to port.

NICOBULUS: That was a wise move. Then what did they do?

CHRYSALUS: They went ashore at sunset.

NICOBULUS: By Hercules, they *did* want to steal our gold! That's what they were up to.

CHRYSALUS: They didn't fool *me*. I knew what they were up to, and it scared me to death. As soon as we saw that they were after our money, we laid our plans right there and then. The next morning we brought the money off the ship and carried it right in front of them in public, in the open, so they would see it.

NICOBULUS: That was clever! Come on, now, what did they do then?

CHRYSALUS: They looked extremely disappointed. As soon as they saw that we were taking the gold with us out of the harbor, they just shook their heads slowly and put their galley back in dock. Then we deposited all the gold with Theotimus, the priest of Diana at Ephesus.

NICOBULUS: Who is this Theotimus?

CHRYSALUS: Oh, *he's* the son of Megalobulus, the dearest man in Ephesus . . . to the Ephesians.

NICOBULUS: If he runs off with all of my gold, he'll be as dear *for* me as he is dear *to* them.

CHRYSALUS: Don't worry, the gold is stored in the temple of Diana. It's under public watch there.

NICOBULUS: You've ruined me! It would be much safer if it were in safekeeping here. Didn't you bring any of the gold home with you?

CHRYSALUS: We did. I don't know how much it was, though.

NICOBULUS: What? You don't know?

CHRYSALUS: Well, you see, Mnesilochus visited Theotimus at night, in secret, and he didn't want to trust me to anyone else on the ship. And so I just don't know how much of a tip he brought with him. But he couldn't have brought very much.

NICOBULUS: You think he could have brought half of it?

CHRYSALUS: Oh, I really don't know, but I don't think so.

NICOBULUS: A third of it?

CHRYSALUS: Oh, I don't think so, but I really honestly don't know. In fact the only thing I do know about the gold is . . . that I don't know. Now you'll have to sail there yourself if you want to get your gold home from Theotimus. [*Nicobulus starts to go off*] Oh yes!

NICOBULUS [*returns*]: What is it? What do you want?

CHRYSALUS: Be sure you remember to take your son's ring along with you.

NICOBULUS: Why do I need his ring?

CHRYSALUS: Because we arranged with Theotimus that he would give the gold to the man who brought the ring.

NICOBULUS [*agreeably*]:   I'll remember. That's good advice. [*Again starts to leave; pauses*] But is this Theotimus rich?

CHRYSALUS: Is he *rich*? Why, he has gold soles on his shoes!

NICOBULUS: How can he afford to live so lavishly?

CHRYSALUS: He has so much money he doesn't know what to do with gold.

NICOBULUS: I wish he would give it to me! Who else was there when the money was given to Theotimus?

CHRYSALUS: The whole city. No one at Ephesus doesn't know about it.

NICOBULUS: At least my son acted wisely in that: he gave the gold for safekeeping to a rich man. You can get money from that kind whenever you need it.

CHRYSALUS: *Why, indeed you can.* He won't keep you waiting the least bit. You'll have it the very day you arrive.

NICOBULUS: I thought I had at last escaped a sailor's life, so an old man like me wouldn't have to set sail at this late stage in life. But I see now that I have no other choice, thanks to my dear friend Archidemides. So. [*Starts to leave again*] Where is my son Mnesilochus now?

CHRYSALUS: He's gone off to the forum to greet the gods and his friends.

NICOBULUS: Then I'll head that way and meet him as soon as possible.

[*Exit*]

CHRYSALUS [*solo*]:   There's one man who's weighted down and carrying an overload![13] Not at all a bad web I've started to weave. To supply my master's son in his love affair, I've seen that he'll have as much gold as he wants; he can return as much to his father as he likes. The old man will go off to Ephesus to get his money while we lead a plushy life here— that is, if the old man leaves us behind and doesn't take me and Mnesilochus with him. [*Chuckling*] What a mess I'll make! [*Pauses*] But what will happen when the old man finds out, when he learns that he went off on a wild-goose chase while we spent all his money? What will happen to me then? He'll change my name for me when he returns! At once he'll turn me from Chrysalus into Crossalus! [*Stretches out arms, as if on cross*] I'll run away if that looks the better course. But if I am caught, I'll give him plenty of hard work. He may have whips in the country, but my back is here at home with me. Now I'll tell my young master about this trick to get the gold for him and his girl friend Bacchis.

[*Exit*]

III.I

LYDUS [*from inside Bacchis I's house*]
Ope' wide at once this door to Hades![14]
I beg you, unlock the door!

[*Enters in state of disarray; to audience*]

Yes, a door to Hell and nothing less:
no one comes this way unless he has
abandoned all hope who enters here.
These sisters Bacchis aren't Bacchises, they're Bacchae!

[*Wildly, in tragic style, now as if seeing Aeschylus's Eumenides*]

Keep away from me, ye sisters who suck men's blood!
The whole house is one great gaudy, bawdy trap!

[*Again to audience*]

As soon as I realized that, I delivered myself to the
tender care of my feet.

[*To an invisible Pistoclerus*]

Am I one to keep all this a secret?
Am I one to conceal it from your father, Pistoclerus?
You're not the least bit ashamed of the deeds you've done?
Deeds that make your father and me,
your friends, your relatives, partners in your crimes?
Well, before you can pile one more evil
on top of what you've already done, I'll tell your father.

[*To audience*]

I'm going to clear myself of any blame for this by exposing it to the old man. Then he can drag him as soon as possible out of this filthy latrine.

[*Exit wildly to the forum*]

III.2

[Enter Mnesilochus followed by slaves with baggage; during the following, they dutifully try to applaud each aphorism][15]

MNESILOCHUS *[with great calm, to audience]*

After many a moment of meditation,
I have an important announcement to make.
"That man who is a friend to his friends,
in the *real* sense of the word,
is a man excelled only by the gods themselves."
That's my experience.

[Polite patter of applause; he bows]

After I left Athens for Ephesus—this was nearly two years ago—I sent a letter from Ephesus here to my old pal Pistoclerus, telling him to find my mistress Bacchis. I learn now that he did find her, or so my slave Chrysalus has just told me. *[Laughs]* You know, that's some scheme he's put together to get my father to supply me with fuel for my fires. In my view, "Nothing is more expensive than an ungrateful man."

[A weaker patter of applause from the slaves; he bows]

Yes,
"It's more profitable to pardon those who are against us
than to abandon those who are for us."

[Still weaker applause, but he bows again]

Yes, indeed,
"It's better to be known as a spendthrift than a miser:
good men praise the first sort, but even evil men
find fault with the second."

[One slave half-heartedly claps once, twice, then falls silent; Mnesilochus bows anyway]

Now I must be careful and keep my eyes open.

[Striking bold pose, as if in soliloquy]

Yes, Mnesilochus, here's where you show yourself!
Here's the test of what kind of man you really are.
Bad, good—one or the other.
Just or unjust.

A miser or a spendthrift.
A comrade or a cad.
Just see that you don't let your own slave outdo you
in doing the right thing. Whatever kind of man you are,
you won't be able to hide it.

[Looks down street]

But look!
There's the father and teacher of my old pal!
I'll listen to what they say from here.

[Stands to one side with his slaves]

III.3

[Enter Lydus and Philoxenus]

LYDUS: Now I'll find out what kind of stuff you're made of. Follow me.

PHILOXENUS: Follow you where? Where are you leading me now?

LYDUS: To the woman who has completely ruined and destroyed your one and only son.

PHILOXENUS: There, there, Lydus. "Those who most gently rage do knowledge more acquire." It would be more surprising if a boy that age weren't up to something like that than if he were. [Aside] I did the same sort of thing when I was a young man.

LYDUS: Oh, woe is me! woe is me! This very permissiveness is what ruined him. Why, if it were not for you I could have made him into a man of fine, upstanding character. Now you and your trusting nature have made Pistoclerus—a degenerate!

MNESILOCHUS: Immortal gods! he just said my old pal's name! What's going on? Why is Lydus attacking his master Pistoclerus?

PHILOXENUS: Now, Lydus, every man has to give way to desire once in a while. The time will come when he will hate himself for it. Give him rein. As long as he's careful not to go too far, just let him alone.

LYDUS: No, I won't let him alone! He will not be corrupted as long as I'm alive! But you, you who offer excuses for a child so corrupted, was this the same kind of education you had when you were a young man? [Philoxenus starts to speak; Lydus silences him] I say no! In your first twenty years of life you never had the chance to stick so much as a finger outside the house without your teacher's permission. If you did not reach the exercise ground before sunrise, the trainer made you pay a pretty price when you did. Nor was that all. On top of that disgrace they piled another: the teacher and his pupil were subject to equal shame.

[Loses contact with surrounding world as he warms to his subject]

Oh yes!
Then they got their exercise by running,
by wrestling, by throwing the javelin and the discus;
by boxing, playing ball, jumping—

[Spits line out]

not by working out with whores and their kisses!

[Backs Philoxenus down the stage]

That was how they spent their lives,
not in dank dins of darkness!
Then when you had returned home from the track
and the exercise ground,
you would sit there in your nice, short little tunic
before your teacher. . .

[Stares into distance imagining the short little tunic; suddenly comes back to the point]

If you mispronounced so much as one syllable while you were reading, your hide would be as striped as a zebra's coat.

MNESILOCHUS [aside]:   I can't stand it! My poor old pal has to put up with this, and all on my account! He's suffering this for my sake, the poor thing!

PHILOXENUS: Things are done differently today, Lydus.

LYDUS: Indeed they are! I doubt it not! In the days gone by, a pupil actually held elected office even before he had ceased to listen to his teacher like a good boy. But now even before he's seven years old, if you so much as lay a finger on him, right away the boy smashes his little writing tablet on his teacher's head. When you go to complain to the father, he says to his boy, [Strutting about, imitating the father] "That's my boy! it takes a real man

to stand up to a teacher's abuse!"
Then he calls in the teacher:
"Hey, you worthless old bum,
don't you dare lay a finger on that boy.
He's only showing his spirit!"
That's the verdict. Case dismissed.

[*To audience*]

How can a teacher have any authority under these conditions
if he's the one who gets the whipping?

MNESILOCHUS [*aside*]: Now *there*'s a real complaint for you! It's a
miracle Pistoclerus hasn't beat Lydus to a pulp for talking like
this.

LYDUS [*at last notices Mnesilochus standing to one side*]: Wait! Who is
that standing in front of the house? Oh, Philoxenus! Here's
one person whose favor I would as soon have as I would a
god's.

PHILOXENUS: Who is he?

LYDUS: Mnesilochus. Your boy's old pal. And not at all of the same
caliber as the one lying in bed in that whorehouse! Oh lucky
Nicobulus! To have raised such a fine lad!

PHILOXENUS: Well, how are you, Mnesilochus? I'm delighted to see
you safe and sound.

MNESILOCHUS [*trying to be as dignified as possible, under the circum-
stances*]: And may the gods bless *you*, Philoxenus.

LYDUS [*still carried away about the good old days and thrilled at this sudden
incarnation of his ideals*]: Oh yes, *here*'s the kind of offspring a
father can be proud of! [*Pushes Philoxenus to one side; embraces
Mnesilochus*] He goes off to sea. He takes care of family
business. He looks after the household. He's obedient and
attentive to his father's every wish and command. He's been
Pistoclerus's *old pal* since they were both little boys. There's
not more than three days' difference in their ages, but this
boy is more than thirty years his senior in common sense.

PHILOXENUS: You'd save yourself a lot of trouble if you would stop
ranting about him.

LYDUS: Hush! You fool, you! Why get angry about your son's bad
reputation when he deserves it?

MNESILOCHUS: Lydus, why are you so angry at my old pal and your
pupil?

LYDUS [*collapses on Mnesilochus's shoulder*]: Your old pal is dead and
   done for.
MNESILOCHUS: Oh gods forbid!
LYDUS: It's just as I said. Why, I myself saw him die. I'm not
   reporting something I heard.
MNESILOCHUS: What happened?
LYDUS: He's dying of love for—oh, the shame of it—a courtesan.
MNESILOCHUS [*prudishly shocked*]: You don't mean it!
LYDUS: She's an absolute whirlpool of a woman. Every man she
   comes in contact with, she sucks down out of sight.
MNESILOCHUS: Where does this woman live?
LYDUS: Here.

[*Points to Bacchis I's house*]

MNESILOCHUS: Where do they say she comes from?
LYDUS: From Samos.
MNESILOCHUS: What's her name?
LYDUS: Bacchis.
MNESILOCHUS [*much relieved*]: Oh, well you're wrong, Lydus. I
   know all about this affair. You're wrong to charge Pistoclerus
   with wrongdoing. He doesn't love her himself. Don't believe
   it. He's simply doing a favor for his friend and well-wisher.
   His *old pal.*

[*His eyes mist over at the thought of his "old pal"*]

LYDUS [*without a moment's hesitation*]: Oh, he is, is he? Does doing a
   nice favor for his friend and *old pal* include holding the
   woman in his lap and kissing her? [*Lubriciously*] Is there no
   way he can do this favor except by running his hands all over
   her breasts, and never taking his lips off hers . . . and . . . and
   . . . [*Sputters*] Why, I can't bring myself even to mention the
   other shameful things he did. [*Long pause; Mnesilochus looks
   relieved*] BUT . . . [*Mnesilochus winces*] while I was there, I saw
   him slip his hand under Bacchis's dress. Why say more?
   [*Drools, recovers*] He's done for: my pupil, your old pal, his
   son. For I say "That man is dead in whom all shame has died."
   What need is there of more words? [*Coyly*] If I had wanted to
   watch a little longer, I should have seen more than was
   proper for either him or me.

MNESILOCHUS [*enraged, aside*]:   Well, *old pal,* you've ruined me! Just wait till I get my hands on that woman! You think I won't ruin her? I'd rather die like a dog. It really is true. You can't know who to trust or believe.

LYDUS [*gleefully, to Philoxenus*]:   See there! Observe what agony your son's corruption has brought to his *old pal.*

PHILOXENUS: Mnesilochus, please try to help him control his passions. Save your *old pal* for your sake and my son for mine.

MNESILOCHUS [*grimly*]:   I intend to do just that.

PHILOXENUS [*to Mnesilochus*]:   I entrust the entire burden to you. This way, Lydus.

LYDUS [*reluctantly*]:   Very well, I'm coming. But it would be better to leave me here with him.

PHILOXENUS: He can handle this.

LYDUS [*pauses for one last word of advice*]:   Mnesilochus, watch over him, make him pay for the disgrace he's brought on me, on you, on all his other friends.

[*Philoxenus drags Lydus off*]

III.4[16]

MNESILOCHUS: Now, I don't know who to believe is my worst enemy—my *old pal* or Bacchis. So she wanted him more than me? Well, let her have him. Fine. I'll see that this causes plenty of trouble for . . . me. [*Tries again to be indignant*] May no one even again believe my sacred oath if I don't use everything in my power to . . . to love her. [*Tries again to be angry*] I'll show her she's got one man she can't make a fool of! Why, I'll go home right now and steal something from . . . my father. And I'll give it to her. [*Making one last effort*] Oh, yes, I'll get my revenge in all kinds of ways. I'll drive her right into the street begging . . . drive my father, that is. [*Pauses, head in hands*] But wait. Can I really be acting in my right mind, forecasting what will happen in the future? You see, I think I *do* love her—in fact I *know* I do. But I'd rather outbid a beggar in begging than let her get so much as one fraction of a feather heavier with my money. No, you'll see, she won't make a fool of me and live! I've decided right now to give back every bit of gold to father. Then just let her try all her wiles on me. With me penniless and empty it won't do her any more good to coax me than it would to tell ghost stories to a corpse in a tomb. [*In a brighter mood*] That's it. Fixed and final. I'm returning that money to father. And I'll beg him not to harm Chrysalus . . . for my sake. I'll beg him to be angry for being made a fool of. . .for my sake. It's only fair that I protect the man who told him a lie. . .for my sake. [*With insufferable self-satisfaction, he turns at last to attendants*] You! Follow me!

[*Exeunt to Nicobulus's house*]

III.5
[*Enter Pistoclerus from Bacchis I's house*]

PISTOCLERUS [*to Bacchis I, inside*]:   I'll postpone everything, Bacchis, until I've done what you ordered me to do: I'll find Mnesilochus and bring him to you. [*Starts towards Nicobulus's house*] But I find his delay very strange. Did my message reach him? I'll look for him here. Maybe he's home.

III.6
[*Enter Mnesilochus from Nicobulus's house*]

MNESILOCHUS: I've given father back every bit of his money. I'd like to see her now that I don't have a coin left. How father hated to pardon Chrysalus! But I finally got him not to hold it against him.[17]

PISTOCLERUS [*aside*]:   Isn't this my old pal?

MNESILOCHUS [*aside*]:   Isn't this my enemy I see?

PISTOCLERUS [*aside*]:   Why, it certainly is.

MNESILOCHUS [*aside*]:   It certainly is.

PISTOCLERUS [*aside*]:   I'll go right up to him.

MNESILOCHUS [*aside*]:   I'll head there now.

PISTOCLERUS: Greetings, Mnesilochus.

MNESILOCHUS: Greetings.

PISTOCLERUS: We must have a dinner to celebrate your safe arrival home from overseas.

MNESILOCHUS: I have no desire for a dinner that would upset my appetite.

PISTOCLERUS: Oh dear, has some trouble spoiled your homecoming?

MNESILOCHUS: Yes, the worst possible trouble.

PISTOCLERUS: What caused it?

MNESILOCHUS: A man I thought was my friend up to now.

PISTOCLERUS [*indignant, he launches into a Lydus-like tirade*]: There are quite a few people around like that now, the kind you think are your friends until they are found out to be traitors steeped in treachery. Lying, ready of tongue! Yes, lazy in work, faithless. There's no one whose good fortune they don't envy. Their slothful ways ensure that no one envies them.

MNESILOCHUS [*dryly*]: Well, I see you have a clear idea of their character. But add one more fault: out of their evil ways they create their own evil. They have no friends, all men are their enemies, and when they deceive themselves, the fools think they're deceiving others. That's exactly the behavior of the man I thought was as much a friend to me as I am to myself. He worked as hard as he could to do me as much harm as he could and take every bit of money I had.

PISTOCLERUS [*shocked*]: He must be an absolute villain!

MNESILOCHUS: My opinion exactly.

PISTOCLERUS: I beg you, tell me who it is!

MNESILOCHUS: A man on excellent terms with you. If it weren't for that, I'd ask you to get back at him any way you could.

PISTOCLERUS: Just tell me his name. If I don't get back at him one way or another why, you can call me the most cowardly man on earth!

MNESILOCHUS: He's a scoundrel, but he's also your friend.

PISTOCLERUS: All the more reason to name him! The friendship of a scoundrel means nothing to me.

MNESILOCHUS: I see I have no choice but to say his name. [*Backs up*] Pistoclerus, you have completely destroyed your old pal.

PISTOCLERUS: What did you say?

MNESILOCHUS: What do you mean, "What did you say?" Didn't I write you from Ephesus telling you to find my mistress for me?

PISTOCLERUS: Of course you did, and I found her.

MNESILOCHUS: Well, weren't there enough courtesans for you in Athens? Did you have to make love to the very girl I had entrusted to you? Did you have to betray me?

PISTOCLERUS [*incredulous*]: Are you in your right mind?

MNESILOCHUS: I got the whole story from your teacher. Don't deny it. You've ruined me.

PISTOCLERUS [*angrily*]:   Are you saying all this to get me angry?

MNESILOCHUS: Don't you love . . .

PISTOCLERUS: Bacchis? Yes. But listen, there are *two* Bacchises inside here.

MNESILOCHUS: What? two . . .

PISTOCLERUS: And they're sisters.

MNESILOCHUS: You're talking nonsense now and you know it.

PISTOCLERUS: That's enough! If you continue to insult me, I'll throw you over my shoulder and carry you inside.

[*Starts to advance*]

MNESILOCHUS [*backing away*]:   I'll go! I'll go! Just wait.

PISTOCLERUS: I won't wait, and I won't have you accusing me without proof.

MNESILOCHUS: I'm coming, I'm coming.

[*They enter Bacchis I's house*]

IV.1

[*Enter parasite with Boy of Cleomachus*]

PARASITE [*to audience*]:   I am the parasite of that worthless, wicked scoundrel, the soldier who brought his girl friend with him from Samos. Now he's ordered me to go to her and find out whether she's going to give him his money or go home with him. [*To Boy*] Whatever house she's in, knock on the door. [*Boy is timid*] Well, go to the door! [*Boy gives a timid knock*] Back off, out of the way! [*To audience*] See how the little rascal knocks? [*To Boy*] You know how to eat a loaf of bread three feet long, but you don't know how to knock on a door! [*Pushes Boy aside; knocks loudly on the door*] Is anyone home? Hey, is anybody inside? Will someone open the door? Is anyone coming?

[*Boy joins in; there arises a horrendous racket*]

IV.2

[*Pistoclerus enters*]

PISTOCLERUS: What is this? Why all this knocking? Why, you little wretch! Why are you wearing out your knuckles on our door? You've nearly knocked it down! What do you want?

PARASITE [*calmly*]:   Hello, young man.

PISTOCLERUS: Hello. Who are you looking for? Who do you want?

PARASITE: Bacchis.

PISTOCLERUS: Which one?

PARASITE [*in a superior way*]:   All I know is, Bacchis. To make a long story short, the soldier Cleomachus sent me to her with the order that she either return his two hundred gold coins or else return with him today to Elatea.

PISTOCLERUS: She's not going. She isn't allowed to go. Go back and deliver that message. She loves another man, not him. Now, off the premises!

PARASITE [*calmly*]:   You seem to be upset.

PISTOCLERUS: And you know why I'm so upset? That face of yours is about one instant away from a beating. See how this dental demolition is twitching?

[*He thrusts both fists in Parasite's face*]

PARASITE [*turns aside, to audience*]:   If I grasp his meaning correctly, I had better be careful he doesn't knock my teeth out. That would mean my dinner's demolition. [*Crosses stage; turns back to Pistoclerus*] Very well, then, I'll tell him. It's you who's in danger.

PISTOCLERUS: What did you say?

[*Advances*]

PARASITE: I'll tell him what you said.

PISTOCLERUS: "Him"? Tell me, who are you?

PARASITE [*self-importantly*]:   I am the armor plating of his body.

PISTOCLERUS: He really must be worthless to have a wretch like you for his armor plating.

PARASITE: He'll be in a soufflé of a rage when he gets here.

PISTOCLERUS: Fine, I hope he collapses.

PARASITE [*going*]:   Anything else you need?

PISTOCLERUS: Yes, go! And you'd better be quick about it.

PARASITE: Good day, Dental Demolator.

PISTOCLERUS: And you, Armor Plate, good-by. [*Parasite and Boy scamper off*] Now things have gotten to the point where I don't know what advice I should give my old pal about his girl friend. He got all angry and paid back all the money to his father, and now he doesn't have one coin to pay back to the soldier. [*The door of Nicobulus's house opens*] But I'd better step to one side here: someone's coming out. [*Enter Mnesilochus, dejected*] Why, look! It's poor old Mnesilochus himself coming out.

IV.3

MNESILOCHUS [*croons*]

Here am I,
Oh so hasty in my heart,
petulant,
Oh so reckless, oh so mad,
with a head out of control,
not in tune, not in style,
here am I.
Here I am,
without honor, without right,
without trust, in a fight,
no one else to love,
no one to love me,
my love affair gone sour,
here am I.

[*To audience*]

Can you believe all this?

[*Resumes character; rapidly*]

I'm everything I wish someone else was!
There's not a more worthless man alive
not one less worthy of the gods' kindness,
not one less worthy of anyone else's company or love.
Enemies are what I should have, not friends;
bad people should help me, not good people.
No man on earth deserves a worse reputation;
it's the only fair reward for a fool like me.
Love made me give my father all his money back,
all that gold I had in my hand.

[*To audience*]

Have you ever seen a worse fool than me? I ruined myself
and I undid everything Chrysalus did for me.

PISTOCLERUS [*aside*]:   I should console him. I'll go to him now. [*To Mnesilochus*] Mnesilochus, how are things?

MNESILOCHUS: I'm ruined!

PISTOCLERUS: Oh gods! Say it's not so!

MNESILOCHUS: I'm ruined!

PISTOCLERUS: Will you be quiet, you fool?

MNESILOCHUS [*shocked at an idea he finds incomprehensible*]:   Be quiet? Me?

PISTOCLERUS: You're clearly not in your right mind.

MNESILOCHUS: I'm ruined! You can't imagine how many woes are crowding in on me, each one sharper and nastier than the last. To think that I could have believed those charges! I had no right to be angry at you.

PISTOCLERUS [*wearily*]:   Oh, cheer up.

MNESILOCHUS [*clearly relishing the self-pity*]:   How can I cheer up? A dead man is worth more than me.

PISTOCLERUS [*making one last effort*]:   The soldier's parasite was just here asking for his money. I drove him away from here, away from the house and the woman. I kicked him out with plenty of tough talk.

MNESILOCHUS: What good does that do *me*? Poor *me*! I can't do a thing. He'll take her away, I just know it.

PISTOCLERUS [*in exasperation*]:   Well, if I had the money, I wouldn't give it to *you*!

MNESILOCHUS: Oh yes you would! I know you. If you weren't in love yourself, I wouldn't trust you so much. As it is, you have more than enough of your own troubles to worry about. I have nothing, but what kind of help can I expect from a man who has nothing?

PISTOCLERUS: Oh, shut up! Some god or other will look out for us.

MNESILOCHUS: Nonsense!

PISTOCLERUS: Wait a minute.

MNESILOCHUS: What is it?

PISTOCLERUS: I see your banker Chrysalus!

IV.4

[*Enter Chrysalus, very pleased with himself*]

CHRYSALUS

Here is one man worth his weight in gold, a fellow worth setting up a gold statue to. I've done a double deed this day,

and I'm off with double spoils. I made my old master play the
fool. What a game he played!
Clever though the old man be,
more clever snares have snared him,
impelled him and compelled him
to trust every word I say.
I've won a royal ransom,
I've rained a golden shower
on the old man's son. You know,
the young boy in love?
the one I eat with?
the one I drink with?
the one whose indoor wherewithal
supports his next-door whorewithall?

Oh, you timid slaves in Greek comedy, you're not for me![18]
You only earn two or three minas of gold for your masters.
What could be more worthless than a slave without a plot?
You're no good unless you have a powerful brain.
If you need a plot, find it in your head.

No man's worth his salt
unless he knows how to be good *and* bad.
He has to be wicked with the wicked,
be a bandit with bandits.
He has to steal where he has to.
The man who knows his trade
knows how to change his skin.
Let him look good to good people
and bad to bad people.
Whatever the moment calls for,
he's ready and willing and able.

[*Returns to the business at hand*]

Well, now, I would like to know just how much gold Mnesilochus skimmed off for himself and how much he returned to
his father. If he has sense, he'll treat Nicobulus like Hercules:
give one part and keep the other nine for himself. [*At last he
sees Mnesilochus and Pistoclerus*] Well, well! Here's the very
fellow I was looking for. Oh master . . . [*They say nothing*] Why

are you two staring at the ground? Did you drop some money? [*Both continue to mope and moon*] What are you so sad and gloomy about? [*Aside to audience*] I don't like this. There has to be a reason for this. [*Still no reply*] Why don't you answer me?

MNESILOCHUS: Chrysalus, I'm a dead man!

CHRYSALUS: Oh, is that all? Maybe you didn't keep enough of the gold for yourself?

MNESILOCHUS: You're damned right I didn't keep enough; in fact, I kept a lot, lot less than enough.

CHRYSALUS: WHAT? You nitwit! When it was *my* courage that let you skim off as little or as much as you pleased? Well, what did you do? Did you carry off only what you could hold by two teeny little fingertips? Didn't you know that an opportunity like this one doesn't often come your way?

MNESILOCHUS: That's not the problem.

CHRYSALUS: Then the problem is that you didn't skim enough off.

MNESILOCHUS: You'll have even more to blame me for once you know what else happened. I'm a dead man.

CHRYSALUS [*aside to audience*]:   Those words tell me there's something worse to come.

MNESILOCHUS: I'm ruined.

CHRYSALUS: Why?

MNESILOCHUS: Because I handed back every bit of the money to my father.

CHRYSALUS: YOU GAVE IT BACK?

MNESILOCHUS: I gave it back.

CHRYSALUS [*his voice breaking*]:   Not all of it. . . not. . . every. . . bit of it?

MNESILOCHUS: Every. . . bit of it.

CHRYSALUS: WE'RE ALL DEAD MEN! How did it ever come into your head to do such a horrible thing?

MNESILOCHUS: Well, Chrysalus, I heard a false charge that Bacchis and Pistoclerus were plotting against me. I was angry about that, and that's why I gave back all the gold to my father.

CHRYSALUS [*in tears of frustration*]:   What did you tell your father when you gave him the gold?

MNESILOCHUS: I said I got the gold directly from his friend Archidemides.

CHRYSALUS: These words will get Chrysalus criss-crossed on a cross this very day. As soon as he sees me, the old man will drag me off to the public executioner!

MNESILOCHUS: Oh, I persuaded my father. . .

CHRYSALUS [*stepping on line*]:   . . .to do what I just said he'd do, right?

MNESILOCHUS: No, no, not at all: *not* to harm you or be angry with you about it. [*Instantly turns sweet*] I barely managed to do it, too. Now *you* have to do something about all this, Chrysalus.

CHRYSALUS: What do you want me to do?

MNESILOCHUS: I want you to lay down another highway to the old man. I want you to lie, create whatever plot you please, concoct some clever fabrication to trick my clever father and make off with his gold.

CHRYSALUS: I don't see how it can be done.

MNESILOCHUS: Oh, go on! *You* can do it. No problem.

CHRYSALUS: NO PROBLEM? Damn it all! Make a fool of a man who just caught me in a lie? He wouldn't believe a word I said. The only way he'll believe me is if I tell him *not* to believe me.

MNESILOCHUS [*picking up this line with interest*]:   Ah, well. . .if only you could hear what he said about you.

CHRYSALUS: What did he say?

MNESILOCHUS [*points up to the sky*]:   He said that if you told him that the sun was the sun, he'd believe it was the moon, and that if you told him it was daylight, he'd know for sure it was really night![19]

CHRYSALUS: Then I will swindle him again today! [*Aside, calmly*] I don't want him to be accused of exaggeration.

MNESILOCHUS: Now what do you want *us* to do?

CHRYSALUS: Absolutely nothing but make love. And that's an order. One more thing: tell me how much gold you need. I'll give it to you. What's the good of having a golden name like Chrysalus if you can't live up to it? Now, tell me, Mnesilochus, just what teeny sum do you need?

MNESILOCHUS: I've got to have two hundred gold coins now to buy Bacchis back from the soldier.

CHRYSALUS: Consider it done.

MNESILOCHUS [*eyes glazing over as all his troubles recede*]:   Well. . .then we'll need an expense account.

CHRYSALUS: No, I'd rather do one thing at a time. First this plot, then the next one. I'll train my catapult on the old man for the two hundred. If I can shatter his towers and breastwork with that charge, then I'll go through the smashed gate into the old, ancient city. Once it's fallen, you and your friend can carry off his gold by the basketful, as much as your heart desires.

PISTOCLERUS: Our lives are in your hands, Chrysalus.

CHRYSALUS: Now, Pistoclerus, go inside to Bacchis and bring out. . .

PISTOCLERUS [*salutes*]: . . . what?

CHRYSALUS: . . . a stylus, wax, tablets, and string.

PISTOCLERUS: I'll do it right now.

[*Salutes; runs into Bacchis I's house*]

MNESILOCHUS: What are you going to do? Tell me!

CHRYSALUS: Is dinner ready? How many are coming? Pistoclerus, you and your girl friend?

MNESILOCHUS: That's right.

CHRYSALUS: There's no woman for Pistoclerus?

MNESILOCHUS: Oh, yes. He's in love with one sister Bacchis, and I'm in love with the other; that adds up to two Bacchises.

CHRYSALUS: What's this?

MNESILOCHUS: Just the lay of the land.

CHRYSALUS: Then where is this twin-sized dining couch of yours?

MNESILOCHUS: Why do you want to know?

CHRYSALUS: It's my business to know. You have no idea what I'm going to do; you don't know what a huge scheme I've got under way.

MNESILOCHUS [*Chrysalus follows*]: Very well, give me your hand and follow me to the door. [*They stand outside Bacchis I's house*] Now look inside.

CHRYSALUS [*a leg dangles out the door*]: Wow! Too sweet for words! Just what I've always wanted!

[*Pistoclerus reenters with tablets, etc.*]

PISTOCLERUS: As you ordered, sir. [*Salutes*] A good order carried out by a good man.

CHRYSALUS: What do you have here?

PISTOCLERUS: Everything you commanded me to bring.

CHRYSALUS [*to Mnesilochus*]: You there, take the stylus and the tablets.

[*Pistoclerus holds the tablets while Mnesilochus writes*]

MNESILOCHUS: Then what?

CHRYSALUS: Write down exactly what I tell you to. I want you to do the writing so your father will recognize your hand when he reads it.

MNESILOCHUS: What should I write?

CHRYSALUS: Greetings and good health to your father, but in your own words.

PISTOCLERUS: Wouldn't it be better for him to write "sickness and death"? That would be more to the point.

CHRYSALUS: No interruptions!

MNESILOCHUS [*labors away, mindless and diligent*]: I've got that order down now.

CHRYSALUS: How does it go?

MNESILOCHUS [*stands up; reads proudly*]: "From: Mnesilochus. To: Father. Subject: Greetings."

CHRYSALUS [*winces*]: Now quick, add this: [*In a huge rush*] "Chrysalus keeps nagging me all the time, Father. He's not nice because I gave your gold back to you and I didn't swindle you."

PISTOCLERUS: Give him time to get it down.

CHRYSALUS: A lover's hand should be quick.

PISTOCLERUS: His hand should be faster at spending money than at writing about it.

PISTOCLERUS: All right, that's down.

CHRYSALUS [*continuing to dictate*]: "Now, dear Father, be on your guard. He's putting together a regular Greek swindle to cheat you out of your gold. *And* he's admitted openly that he'll take it." Now, write that out plain and direct.

MNESILOCHUS [*after a moment*]: All right, go on.

CHRYSALUS: "*And* he promises that he's going to give it to me so I can give it all to whores and gobble it up like a degenerate Greek, Father. *But*, Father, watch out: don't let him make a fool of you today. Please, *please* be careful."

MNESILOCHUS [*finishes*]: Go on. What next?

CHRYSALUS: Just add . . . h'm . . .

[*Pauses*]

MNESILOCHUS: Tell me what to write.

CHRYSALUS: Ah! "*But*, Father, *please* remember what you promised me: don't beat him. Just tie him up and keep him at home under guard." [To Pistoclerus] You, give us the wax and string. [To Mnesilochus] Come on, fasten it and seal it, quick!

MNESILOCHUS [looks blank]: Now will you please tell me what good all of this is going to do? Why are you telling him not to trust you and to tie you up and stand watch over you at home?

CHRYSALUS: Because I want to tell him, that's why. You mind your own business and leave mine alone! My solid references got me this job. I'm the one taking all the risks.

MNESILOCHUS: Fair enough.

CHRYSALUS: Hand over the letter.

MNESILOCHUS: There you are.

CHRYSALUS: Now, pay attention, Mnesilochus, and you too, Pistoclerus. Both of you go now into the dining room. Take your places on that twin-sized couch of yours. Once you're set up there, your job is to start drinking. That's an order.

PISTOCLERUS: Any more orders?

CHRYSALUS: One more: once you've taken your places, don't dare leave unless you get a signal from me.

PISTOCLERUS: Oh noble general!

CHRYSALUS: You're still here? You could have had *two* drinks by now!

PISTOCLERUS: We're *running*!

CHRYSALUS: You tend to your business. I'll busy myself with mine.

[They both double-time into Bacchis I's house]

IV.5

CHRYSALUS [solo]: What a monstrous concoction of a plot I've got brewing! My only worry is that I may not be able to make the plot work. The first thing I've got to do is get the old man mad and raging at me. It wouldn't be a proper Greek swindle if he saw me in a tranquil, gentle mood. I'll have him turned inside-out today, stake my life on it. I'll roast him dry as a parched pea.

Now to stroll to his door! When he comes out, I'll be well placed to put the letter in his hand.

IV.6

[Nicobulus comes rushing out of his house]

NICOBULUS: What an outrage to me and my dignity! That Chrysalus has got away from me!

CHRYSALUS [aside]: I'm saved! The old man is angry. Now's the time for me to go up to him.

NICOBULUS: Who is that talking over there? Why, I believe it's Chrysalus!

CHRYSALUS: Here goes.

NICOBULUS [sarcastically]: Oh excellent slave, greetings. How are things? How soon should I set sail for Ephesus to bring back my gold from Theotimus? [Chrysalus does not respond] Nothing to say? I swear by all the gods that if I didn't love my son so and want to give him anything he asks for, your hide would have been well whipped by now. You could spend the rest of your life in chains at the mill. I've learned all about your crimes from Mnesilochus.

CHRYSALUS [innocently]: He's charged me? [aside] That's perfect! I'm the one that's wicked and the scoundrel. You just watch what happens! I won't say another word.

NICOBULUS: You cut-throat! Are you making threats?

CHRYSALUS: You'll know soon enough what kind of person he is. He ordered me to bring you this letter. He asked that you do whatever is written here.

NICOBULUS: Hand it over.

CHRYSALUS: Notice the seal.

NICOBULUS: I do. Where is he?

CHRYSALUS: I don't know. [Aside] The only proper thing for me is to know nothing. I've forgotten everything. [To Nicobulus] You know that I'm a slave. I don't even know what I do know. [Aside] Now the little birdie has seen the worm and walked into the trap. With the noose I've set, I'll have this fellow hung up nicely.

NICOBULUS: Just a moment. [Reads the letter] AARGH! I'll soon come back to you, Chrysalus.

[Goes back into his house]

CHRYSALUS: As if he were playing the trick on me! As if I didn't know what he's going to do! He's gone inside to get some slaves to tie me up. But it's his ship of state that's floundering nicely; my little bark is sailing along fine. Now I'll quiet down. I hear the door opening.

IV.7

[*Enter Nicobulus with his slaves overseer Artamo and other slaves*]

NICOBULUS: Now, Artamo, seize that fellow there and tie him up.

[*Artamo and company do so*]

CHRYSALUS [*feigns innocence*]: What have I done?

NICOBULUS [*to Artamo*]: Smash him in the face if he lets out a peep! [*To Chrysalus*] What does this letter say?

CHRYSALUS: Why are you asking me? I took it from him and brought it all sealed to you.

NICOBULUS: Oh, you rascal, you! You've been berating my son because he gave the gold back to me? And you said that you would use some Greek swindle to get the money from me?

CHRYSALUS [*all innocence*]: *I* said *that*?

NICOBULUS: Yes.

CHRYSALUS: Who is it said that I said that?

NICOBULUS: Quiet! [*Artamo hits Chrysalus*] No man said it. The letter you brought here indicts you. [*Points to the letter*] See! These words order you to be tied up.

CHRYSALUS [*takes letter, pretends to read very carefully*]: Aha! Your son has made me the courier of my own death warrant, just like Bellerophon.[20] So I brought the very letter that orders me to be tied up? Very well. So what?

NICOBULUS: I'm only doing this to make you persuade my son that he ought not to live like a degenerate Greek, you wretched swine.

CHRYSALUS: Oh, you fool, you fool! Here you are, standing on the block, the slave-dealer is calling out your name, and you don't even know that you're on sale.

NICOBULUS: Tell me, who is selling me?

CHRYSALUS [*to audience*]: As the poet says,
"He whom the gods love dies young,
while he still has his strength, sense, and wit."

[*Points to Nicobulus*]

If any god loved this man, he would have died more than ten years ago—no, more than twenty years ago. This burden on the earth walks around and knows nothing, feels nothing. He's as worthless as a rotten mushroom.

NICOBULUS [*to Chrysalus*]: So, I'm a burden on the earth, you say?

[*To Artamo*] Take him inside and string him up tight to the whipping post. You'll never take my gold away from me!

CHRYSALUS: Ha! You'll soon give it away.

NICOBULUS: Give it away?

CHRYSALUS: Yes, and you yourself will beg me to take it away, when you find out the deadly danger my accuser is in . . . [*Ominously*] . . . Oh how much deadly danger. Then you'll shower liberty all over Chrysalus, but I'll never take it.

NICOBULUS: Tell me, you piece of trash, what kind of danger is my son Mnesilochus in?

CHRYSALUS: Follow me this way and you'll find out soon enough.

NICOBULUS [*following Chrysalus*]: Where in the world are we going?

CHRYSALUS: Just three steps.

NICOBULUS: More like ten.

[*They go over to Bacchis I's door*]

CHRYSALUS: Come now, Artamo, open this door just a teeny little crack. Softly! No squeaks! [*The door is opened a crack*] Now, that's enough. [*To Nicobulus*] Come here, you. You see the banquet going on inside?

[*Sounds of drunken orgy*]

NICOBULUS [*peers in; door is closed*]: I saw Pistoclerus lying opposite Bacchis!

CHRYSALUS: And who is on the other couch?

NICOBULUS [*peers in again*]: Oh no! I'm destroyed!

CHRYSALUS: You know the fellow?

NICOBULUS: I know him.

CHRYSALUS: Now, please give me your opinion: isn't she beautiful?

NICOBULUS: Very much so.

CHRYSALUS: And do you think she's a courtesan?

NICOBULUS: What else?

CHRYSALUS: You couldn't be more wrong.

NICOBULUS: Then, for God's sake, who is she?

CHRYSALUS [*mysteriously*]: You'll find out soon enough. . . but not from me. . . and not today.

IV.8

[*Without warning, the soldier Cleomachus enters. At first he does not see the crowd at Bacchis's door*]

CLEOMACHUS [to audience]

so! It's Mnesilochus, son of Nicobulus, who keeps
my woman here by force? What are his intentions?

NICOBULUS [to Chrysalus]:   Who is that?

CHRYSALUS [aside]:   The soldier has come just in time for me.

CLEOMACHUS [continues to speak to audience]

May he think me not a soldier but a woman
who cannot defend myself and those who are mine.
May neither Bellona nor Mars ever again trust me
if I don't render him lifeless when I meet him,
if I don't disinherit him from his living estate!

NICOBULUS: Chrysalus, who is that man who's threatening my son?

CHRYSALUS: Him? Oh, just the husband of the very woman your
son is in bed with!

NICOBULUS: WHAT! Her husband!

CHRYSALUS: That's what I said, her *husband*.

NICOBULUS: Oh no! She's married!

CHRYSALUS: You'll learn for sure soon enough.

NICOBULUS: Poor me! I'm ruined!

CHRYSALUS: Now, then, does Chrysalus seem such a villain to you?
Go ahead, keep me tied up! Just listen to your son. Didn't I
tell you you would find out what kind of man he is?

NICOBULUS: Now what will I do?

CHRYSALUS: Order me to be untied at once. If I'm not untied soon,
he'll catch your son in the act.

CLEOMACHUS [continues to address audience]

Nothing, no sum of money, would give me as much pleasure
as catching him in bed with her! Then I could kill them both!

CHRYSALUS: Did you hear what he said? Are you going to order me
untied or are you not?

NICOBULUS [to Artamo]:   Untie him! I'm scared to death!

CLEOMACHUS [brandishing sword]

I'll show her, that woman who sells her own body to the mob!
This is one man she won't be able to say she made a fool of.

CHRYSALUS [to Nicobulus]:   P-p-p-p-Possibly you could pacify him
with a pittance from your pocket?[21]

NICOBULUS [startled; recovers]:   Well, pacify him any way you please,
just so he doesn't catch my son *in flagrante* and kill him!

CLEOMACHUS [continues to address the world at large]

Unless exactly two hundred gold coins are returned to me at once,
I shall instantly squeeze the breath of life out of both of them!

NICOBULUS: There! Pacify him now, if you can.

CHRYSALUS: I'll do exactly that. [*Goes over to Cleomachus; shouts*] WHY ARE YOU SHOUTING?

CLEOMACHUS [*at last notices others on stage*]: Where is your master?

CHRYSALUS [*for Nicobulus's benefit*]: NOWHERE. I don't know. [*Whispers to Cleomachus*] Do you want two hundred gold coins right now, on the condition that you don't make a noise or uproar here?

CLEOMACHUS: There's nothing I would more prefer.

CHRYSALUS [*aside only to Cleomachus*]: And on the condition that I can use harsh language with you?

CLEOMACHUS [*nods assent*]: As you think best.

NICOBULUS [*completely misreading their gestures*]: See how that murderer is giving in!

CHRYSALUS [*whispers*]: That's the father of Mnesilochus. Follow me. He'll promise it to you. Ask for your gold. As for the rest, [*Loudly so Nicobulus hears*] A WORD TO THE WISE IS SUFFICIENT.

NICOBULUS: Well? now what?

CHRYSALUS: I've made a settlement for two hundred gold coins.

NICOBULUS: Oh my salvation! You've saved me! How soon should I say "I'll pay"?

[*Embraces Chrysalus's knees*]

CHRYSALUS [*lifts Nicobulus up; turns to Cleomachus*]: You make your demand. [*Cleomachus kneels; to Nicobulus*] And *you* swear your oath.

[*Nicobulus kneels*]

NICOBULUS: All right, I swear. [*To Cleomachus*] Now make your demand.

CLEOMACHUS: Will you give me two hundred genuine gold coins?

CHRYSALUS [*to Nicobulus, raising him*]: Now answer him. Say "I do."

NICOBULUS: I do.

[*Cleomachus rises also*]

CHRYSALUS [*turning on Cleomachus for a mock tirade*]:   Now what, you
scurvy dog? Is anything else due you? [*Backs Cleomachus across
stage*] Why are you upsetting him? Why are you threatening
him with death? He and I will see that you pay for this! You
have a sword here, but we have a spit inside. You get me mad
enough at you and I'll puncture you with more holes than a
mouse in a mousetrap. So help me, I know what's been
bothering you so. You think Mnesilochus is inside with that
woman!
CLEOMACHUS: *Think* he is? I *know* he is!
CHRYSALUS [*raising his hands in prayer to heaven*]
So help me
JUPITER, JUNO, CERES, MINERVA, LATONA,
SPES, OPIS, VIRTUS, VENUS,
CASTOR, POLLUX, MARS, MERCURY, HERCULES,
SUMMANUS, SOL, SATURN[22]
—and any other gods that happen to be around—
he's not lying down with her,
he's not walking alongside her,
he's not listening to her,
he's not doing anything to her
they said he was doing to her!

[*Collapses in a faint in Nicobulus's arms*]

NICOBULUS [*thrilled, to audience*]:   What an oath! He's saved me by
his perjury!
CLEOMACHUS: Then where *is* Mnesilochus?
CHRYSALUS: His father sent him to the country. As for Bacchis,
why, she's gone up to the Acropolis to look at the Parthenon.
It's open, you know. Go and see if she's not there.
CLEOMACHUS: Well, then, I'll go to the forum.
CHRYSALUS [*aside*]:   Or to hell.
CLEOMACHUS [*turns back*]:   I do get the gold today, right?
CHRYSALUS: Get it and be hanged! Don't think he's going to beg you
for anything today! [*Exeunt Cleomachus and attendants*] He's
off, and good riddance. [*To Nicobulus*] By the gods, sir, let me
go inside to your son.
NICOBULUS: Inside? Why do you want to go inside?

CHRYSALUS: I intend to give him a good dressing down, in detail, for putting us to all this trouble.

NICOBULUS: Oh, please *do*, Chrysalus! Don't spare him a single word!

CHRYSALUS: *You*'re telling me what to do? When he's going to hear more mouthing from me today than Socrates ever heard from Xanthippe?[23]

[*Runs into Bacchis I's house*]

NICOBULUS [*to audience*]:   That slave is exactly like a sore eye: if he's not there, you don't want him and you don't need him; if he *is* there, you can't keep your hands off him. If he hadn't had the good luck to be here today, that soldier would have caught Mnesilochus with his wife. He would have hacked him into little pieces for his adultery. It's as if—in a manner of speaking—I've bought my own son for the two hundred coins I promised the soldier. But I won't pay them out rashly until I've had a chance to see my son. I'll never put rash trust in Chrysalus. Still, I think I might read this letter over again. You can always trust signed and sealed letters.

[*Goes off towards the forum but pauses; remains onstage throughout the following scene*]

IV.9
[*Enter Chrysalus from Bacchis I's house*]
CHRYSALUS [*declaims in epic style*][24]

OF ATREUS'S TWO SONS, THOSE BROTHERS WHO NAME
DID MOST IMMORTAL WIN, WHEN LAST WAS RAZED
PROUD PRIAM'S PATRIOTIC PERGAMUM
DESTROYED THOUGH FORTIFIED BY HAND DIVINE—
THROUGH FELL SWORDS, HORSE, AND HELLAS' WARRIORS ALL
ILLUSTRIOUS, WITH A THOUSAND SHIPS BESIDES,
IN SIEGE PERMÁNENT FULL TEN YEARS...I sing.

[*Briskly, cheerfully*]

All that was no more than a stubbed toe compared with the siege I've laid on Nicobulus: a siege without ships and army, without a single soldier. [*Looks around the stage, does not see Nicobulus, who is present during the entire "Song of Troy"*] Ah, I have time for one dirge before he returns.

[Falls to one knee; sings]

> *Oh Troy my enemy,*
> *My country 'tis of thee,*
> *Oh Pergamum,*
> *Oh Priam 'bout to die,*
> *In twinkling of an eye,*
> *Old man who lost four hundred coins,*
> *Of thee I sing.*

[Stands up. As he gestures with the letter, he becomes a lecturer in a lecture hall]

Now for a lecture in Greek mythology. You see, this letter which I signed and sealed is no letter: it's the wooden horse the Greeks left at Troy. Pistoclerus is its architect Epius, Mnesilochus is the traitor Sinon, left behind to trick the Trojans. Instead of Achilles' tomb, there's Bacchis's bed: no signal fires here to summon Greeks, just fires of passion. This Sinon is burning *himself* up. And I'm the Ulysses who concocted the whole scheme. So the words written here aren't really words, but Greeks armed and hiding inside the Trojan horse. That's where our plot stands at the moment. Our horse will make its charge on a strongbox instead of a stronghold: an exquisite equestrian extinction[25] for the old man and his gold. *[Points to the door of Nicobulus's house]* Now, think of the old fool Nicobulus as the city Troy, and say the soldier Cleomachus is Menelaus; that leaves the roles of Agamemnon and Ulysses to me alone. Then Mnesilochus plays Paris, the boy who caused his country's ruin. He ran off with Helen, see, and that's why I had to lay siege to Troy. Now about Ulysses. From what I've heard, he was as bad and bold as me. I was nearly tricked by my own tricks, and so was he when he went on a reconnaissance tour of Troy. But he tricked his way out of Troy, and so did I: I was tied up, but my tricks untied me the same day.

[Staggers backwards as the Muse's inspiration strikes again]

THREE EPIC PORTENTS OF TROY'S DOOM WERE TOLD:
IF THE CITADEL OF A GODDESS STATUE[26]
WAS BEREFT; IF TROILUS, PRIAM'S SON,
DID DIE; IF PHRYGIAN GATE BY TROJAN HORSE

WAS FROM ITS HINGE DISCHARGED . . . I sing.
Well, that was that.

[Returns to the lecture platform]

That's good. Very good. Now for the commentary. There are
three portents that apply to our Troy, too. A little while ago,
when I told the old man that lie about his girl friend and the
gold and the galley, that was stealing Athena's statue from the
citadel. That left two portents to go—I didn't have the town
yet. When I took the letter to the old man, that was killing
Troilus. He thought that Mnesilochus had been with the wife
of the soldier. After that, I locked in struggle with the soldier
Cleomachus, the kind who takes a city with words instead of
arms. I beat him back. Then I closed for a fight with the old
man. With one lie I beat him to his knees, with one quick blow
I stripped him of his spoils. Now he's given two hundred gold
coins to the soldier, as he promised, but I need two hundred
more. After all, our soldiers need wine and honey to celebrate
the fall of Troy. But *this* Priam is a lot better than the one in
Homer. He had only fifty sons, but ours has four hundred,
and each one is in absolutely mint condition. I'll dispatch
every one of them today, with just two blows. *[Advances to
audience]* Is there any buyer for this Priam of mine? A real
bargain. I'll sell him as soon as I take the town by storm.
[Nicobulus turns back towards his house] But look! There's Priam
himself in front of his house! I'll go over and talk to him.

NICOBULUS *[looks furtively about]*:   Someone's speaking nearby. I
wonder who?

CHRYSALUS: Oh Nicobulus . . .

NICOBULUS: What's going on? Have you done what I sent you to
do?

CHRYSALUS: You ask? Come over here.

NICOBULUS: Here I am.

CHRYSALUS: Outstanding orator, that's me. I reduced the boy to
tears. I pointed out all his faults. I cursed him. I used everything I could think of.

NICOBULUS: What did he say?

CHRYSALUS *[sighs heavily]*:   Oh, he didn't say a word. He stood there
silent . . . weeping . . . listening to everything I had to say. He
wrote out a letter . . . still silent . . . he sealed it . . . gave it to

me. He ordered me to give it to you, but I'm afraid you'll sing the same song you sang before. Look at that seal. Is it his?

NICOBULUS: That's it. I'd like to read this.

CHRYSALUS: Oh, please *do*. [*Hands it over; aside*] Now the Phrygian gate is down. Now for the fall of Troy! My Trojan-horse trick is working nicely.

NICOBULUS: Chrysalus, stay here while I read this letter.

CHRYSALUS: Why do I need to stay with you?

NICOBULUS: I want you to know what the letter says so that you can do what I order you to.

CHRYSALUS: I'm not going to stay, and I don't want to know.

NICOBULUS: No matter. Stay here.

CHRYSALUS: Stay here? What's the need?

NICOBULUS: The need is that you keep quiet and do what I tell you to.

CHRYSALUS: I'm here, I'm here.

NICOBULUS [*opens letter*]: Oh, what tiny little letters!

CHRYSALUS: They're small for someone whose eyesight is poor, but they're big enough for anyone who can see well.

NICOBULUS: Then pay attention.

CHRYSALUS: I said I don't want to!

NICOBULUS: And I said I want you to!

CHRYSALUS [*as before*]: What's the need?

NICOBULUS: The need is for you to do what I order you to.

CHRYSALUS: It's only right that your servants serve at your command.

NICOBULUS: Pay attention now.

CHRYSALUS: Read when you are ready. My ears are at your disposal.

NICOBULUS: Gods, he didn't spare the wax or the stylus. But whatever it says, I'm bound to read it through. [*Reads letter*] "Father: please give Chrysalus two hundred gold coins. If you want me safe and sound, that is." Oh no! It's as bad as I thought!

CHRYSALUS: You know...

NICOBULUS: What?

CHRYSALUS: He didn't even say "Dear Father" first!

NICOBULUS [*looks hard at letter*]: I don't see it anywhere.

CHRYSALUS [*indignant*]: You won't pay him a thing, if you're smart; but if you do decide to pay, let him find himself another messenger if *he*'s smart. I'm not carrying anything anywhere, to anybody, no matter how much you order me to. I'm already under enough suspicion as it is, and I haven't done a thing wrong!

NICOBULUS: Listen! There's still more to read here.

CHRYSALUS: And it's an outrageous letter from the very beginning.

NICOBULUS: "I am ashamed to come into your sight, Father. I've heard that you know all about my horrible crime, about my sleeping with the wife of a foreign soldier." He's not joking there! I've saved you from your own sins with two hundred gold coins.

CHRYSALUS: There's nothing new there. You haven't said a thing *I* didn't say to him.

NICOBULUS [*continues*]: "I confess I acted foolishly. *But* please don't desert me in my foolishness, Father. Passion governed my heart; my eyes were not my own to control; I was persuaded to do that which I now am ashamed to confess I have done." Ha! the proper thing would have been for you to have avoided it, rather than be ashamed about it now!

CHRYSALUS: Why, I said the very same thing to him just a while ago!

NICOBULUS [*continues*]: "PLEASE, Father, I beg you to be satisfied with the endless, sound scoldings I got from Chrysalus. His instructions have made a better man of me, so you really ought to be grateful to him for that."

CHRYSALUS [*feigns surprise*]: Why, is *that* what he says?

NICOBULUS: Here! Look! See for yourself.

CHRYSALUS: How easily a guilty man turns suppliant to everyone he meets!

NICOBULUS [*continues*]: "Now if I still have the right to ask you for something, Father, give me two hundred gold coins . . . please . . . pretty please?"

CHRYSALUS: If you're smart, you won't give him a single one!

NICOBULUS [*exasperated*]: Let me finish! "I took an oath in no uncertain terms to give that money back to the woman before nightfall, before she leaves me. Now, Father, please see that I don't perjure myself and get me away from here as soon as you can and see that I escape the clutches of that woman who made me commit so many sins and crimes. Don't be upset over a trifling two hundred gold coins: I'll pay you back six hundred—if I live, that is. I remain, Sincerely yours, your disobedient son Mnesilochus. P.S. Take care of all this right away." Well! what do you think, Chrysalus?

CHRYSALUS [*outraged*]:   Oh no, I'm not about to give *you* any advice today! I'm not about to take a chance of having you say you did something on my advice that later went wrong. BUT . . . if you want my opinion, if I were in your place, I'd give him the money rather than let him be completely ruined. There are two possibilities; the choice is yours: Either you lose your money or he loses his good word. *I*'m not about to order you, or forbid you, or persuade you to do anything.

NICOBULUS [*weakening*]:   I *do* feel sorry for him.

CHRYSALUS: He's your son. Nothing strange in that. If there must be more losses, it's better to accept them than to have his scandals spread all over town.

NICOBULUS: By the gods, I'd rather have him in Ephesus, where he's safe, than have him here at home. But what else is there to do? I'll go ahead and lose what has to be lost. I'll bring out the four hundred gold coins now, both the two hundred I've promised the soldier—poor me—and the other two hundred. Wait here, Chrysalus: I'll be right back.

[*He rushes into his house*]

CHRYSALUS [*solo*]:   Troy is laid waste! The marshals of the host are razing Pergamum! I knew I'd be the ruin of Troy! Whoever says I'm worthy of the worst kind of punishment—well, I wouldn't dream of disagreeing. What a confusing little plot I'm weaving! But the door's opening! The booty is being carried out of Troy. I'll keep quiet now.

[*Enter Nicobulus with two bags of gold*]

NICOBULUS: Take this gold, Chrysalus. Go on, take it to my son. I'm off this way to the forum to pay back the soldier.

CHRYSALUS: Oh no, I absolutely won't take it! You go and find someone else to do it. I don't want this to be entrusted to me!

NICOBULUS: Take it! Don't annoy me.

CHRYSALUS: Oh no, I absolutely won't have it.

NICOBULUS: PLEASE.

CHRYSALUS: I said that's that. And that's *that.*

NICOBULUS: Stop stalling.

[*Hands bags over*]

CHRYSALUS [*begins to relent*]: I said I don't want the gold entrusted to me! Well, at least get somebody to keep guard on me.

NICOBULUS: Aargh! You're getting me angry again.

CHRYSALUS [*seeming to give way reluctantly*]: Give it here, then, if you have to.

NICOBULUS: Now, see to this. I'll be back shortly.

[*Runs off towards forum*]

CHRYSALUS: I'll see to it—[*Pauses until Nicobulus is offstage*]—see that you're the most wretched old fool alive! [*To audience*] This is the way to finish: end with a flourish. How nicely things are going! What a Roman triumph! What a load of spoils! To make it official: [*As if giving an official decree*]

THE PUBLIC SAFETY HAVING BEEN ESTABLISHED,

THE TOWN HAVING BEEN CAPTURED THROUGH GUILE,

I LEAD OUR ARMY UNHARMED AND WHOLE BACK HOME.[27]

But don't be surprised if I don't celebrate a triumph now. They're far too common these days, spectators. My troops will have all the wine and honey they need. Now to carry this booty straight to our quartermaster!

[*Exit into the house of Bacchis I*]

IV.10

[*Enter Philoxenus*]

PHILOXENUS: The more I ponder the turmoils my son is toiling in, the more the ignorant simpleton sinks into his life of hedonistic habits, the more I worry and the more I fear that he'll be compromised and corrupted. I know, I was his age once and I did all those things . . . [*Pauses*] . . . but in a restrained way. I got married, I knew whores, I had too many drinks, I knew all about sex, I paid for all that—but not too often. In fact, I don't much care for the attitude most parents display these days towards their sons. I decided that I would give my son whatever his heart desired. I think that's only fair. Of course, I don't want to give *too much* play to his playing around. [*Goes to Nicobulus's door*] Now I'll see Mnesilochus about my instructions to him, see whether or not his labors have contrived to drive Pistoclerus over to virtue and a rewarding life. I know he would have done that, given the chance. To do so is the nature of the boy.

V.1

[*Nicobulus enters in a rage from the forum. He does not see Philoxenus throughout the following*]

NICOBULUS [*to audience*]

WHOEVER AND WHEREVER THEY ARE,

WHOEVER THEY HAVE BEEN OR WILL BE,

OF ALL THE FOOLISH, FATUOUS, FUNGUS-COVERED,

DUNDERHEADED,

STUPID, DRIVELING, DEHYDRATED DOLTS!

IN STUPIDITY AND MINDLESSNESS I OUTRUN THE PACK.

I'M RUINED! I'M DISGRACED!

How could I be tricked *twice* like this, and at my age? The more I think about the mess my son made, the hotter I get! Ruined and ripped and wracked this way and that! Pursued by every evil known to man, I've died each death there is to die. Chrysalus has chopped me all to bits, and stripped the spoils from poor innocent me. That devil has fleeced me of my gold, and with his anything but innocent ways has done just as he pleased with me! You know what happened? The soldier tells me that the woman is really a courtesan, the woman Chrysalus called his wife! He told me everything else that happened, too. He had hired her out for a year, so the money I paid him—STUPID IDIOT THAT I AM—was only the gold that was the balance due on his account! *That* is what galls me the most of all! The worst torture of all is to be made to play the fool at my age! For me, with my white hair and my snow-white beard, to be picked clean of all my money! I'm ruined. My own slave treats me like dirt! If only I had lost my money some place else! I'd at least be able to endure that better than this!

PHILOXENUS: I'm sure I thought someone was speaking nearby. [*At last he notices Nicobulus*] But who is this? Why, it's the father of Mnesilochus!

NICOBULUS: Oh, just what I needed! There's my partner in toil and trouble. Greetings, Philoxenus.

PHILOXENUS: Same to you. Where are you coming from?

NICOBULUS: The place any wretched, penniless old man should be coming from.

PHILOXENUS: Yes, wretched and penniless men like us deserve to be there.

NICOBULUS: I see. We're as alike in our fortunes as we are in our years.

PHILOXENUS: Just so. But what's *your* trouble?

NICOBULUS: The same as yours.

PHILOXENUS: So! Does your malady have anything to do with your son?

NICOBULUS: You might say so.

PHILOXENUS: I have the same malady.

NICOBULUS: Chrysalus, that excellent fellow, ruined my son, me, and all my wealth.

PHILOXENUS: Please tell me what your son has done to upset you.

NICOBULUS: I'll tell you. He's ruined your son! They both have mistresses!

PHILOXENUS [*recoils*]: How do you know?

NICOBULUS: I saw them.

PHILOXENUS: Oh no! Ruined again!

NICOBULUS: Well, what are we waiting for? Let's both go and knock on the door.

[*Gestures towards Bacchis I's house*]

PHILOXENUS: Excellent idea.

NICOBULUS: Hey! Bacchis! Open this door at once! You'd better open the door now if you don't want to lose your door and doorpost to axes!

[*They both bang*]

V.2

BACCHIS I [*from inside*]:[28] What's the meaning of this uproar? Who is it? Who called?

[*Bacchis I and Bacchis II enter*]

NICOBULUS: This fellow and me.

BACCHIS I [*to Bacchis II*]: What's going on? Goodness, dear, who drove these sheep here?

NICOBULUS: The bitch is calling us sheep!

BACCHIS II: Their shepherd must be taking a nap to let them stray bleating like this away from the flock.

BACCHIS I: Oh dear, they *are* trim and neat, aren't they? They don't seem a bit dirty.

BACCHIS II: Yes indeed, they've both been very well shorn.

PHILOXENUS: Look at them making fun of us!

NICOBULUS: Let them carry on as much as they like.

BACCHIS I [*to Bacchis II*]:   How often would you say they get fleeced? Three times a year?

BACCHIS II [*points to Nicobulus*]:   I think this one was sheared twice today.

BACCHIS I: They are both fleeceless, aren't they?

BACCHIS II: And they used to have such *nice* wool.

BACCHIS I [*sees that Philoxenus and Nicobulus are more interested than indignant*]:   Now, I ask you, just look at those sidelong stares.

BACCHIS II: I don't think they mean anything nasty by it.

PHILOXENUS [*to Nicobulus*]:   This is just what we deserve for coming here!

BACCHIS I: They ought to be driven inside.

BACCHIS II: What good would it do? They don't have any milk or wool. Let them stand here. They've given as much as they can. All the fruit has dropped from their branches anyway. [*Stares suggestively at the two men*] Don't you see how they're wandering around untended? Why, I believe they're dumb with age. They don't let out so much as one bleat when they're apart from their flock. They just seem stupid, not bad.

[*Laughs*]

BACCHIS I: Let's go back inside, sister.

[*They turn to go*]

NICOBULUS: Both of you stay right there! These *sheep* want you.

BACCHIS II: This is indeed a miracle! These sheep are addressing us in human speech!

PHILOXENUS: This is *one* pair of sheep that's going to bite the hand that sheared them!

BACCHIS I [*briskly*]:   If you have a debt, I hereby cancel it. Keep the money, I'll never ask for it. What possible excuse could you have to threaten us in so unsheeplike a fashion?

PHILOXENUS: Because you have our two little lambs fenced inside your house.

NICOBULUS: Besides those lambs, you have my watchdog too! Unless you lead them outside this instant, we'll turn into rams and butt you right down.

BACCHIS I: Sister, there's something I must say to you in private.

BACCHIS II: Do tell me what it is.

[*They draw to one side*]

NICOBULUS: Where are they going?

BACCHIS I [*with Bacchis II, off to one side of stage*]:   I'm putting you in charge of that old man. [*Points to Philoxenus*] You calm him down. I'll take the one that's angry, and we'll both see if we can't persuade them to come inside.

BACCHIS II: I'll play my part as well as I can, but it is revolting to lie in the arms of a dead man.

BACCHIS I: Well, get to it.

BACCHIS II: Hush! You see to your job and I'll do mine.

NICOBULUS: What plot are those two hatching in secret over there?

PHILOXENUS: Uh . . . Nicobulus.

NICOBULUS: Yes?

PHILOXENUS: There's something embarrassing I've got to tell you.

NICOBULUS: What is it that's so embarrassing?

PHILOXENUS [*pauses, then goes ahead*]:   All right, here goes. I'm going to confess, my loyal friend. I'm worthless.

NICOBULUS: Oh well, I've known that for some time. But why are you worthless? Come on, tell me.

PHILOXENUS [*straining towards Bacchis I and Bacchis II, in romantic tones*]
I'm adrift on a swelling tide of passion . . .
my heart's pierced through and through . . .

NICOBULUS [*disgusted*]
It would be more in your fashion
to have your old *ass* pierced, too.[29]

[*Philoxenus is shocked out of his reverie*]

What do you mean? Even though I already probably know what you're going to say, I'd prefer to hear it from you.

PHILOXENUS [*points to Bacchis II, who is parading alluringly*]:   See her?

NICOBULUS: Yes.

PHILOXENUS: She's really not so bad . . .

NICOBULUS: Oh yes she is, and you *are* indeed worthless!

PHILOXENUS: Why say more? I'M IN LOVE!

[*Dashes over to her*]

NICOBULUS: YOU? IN LOVE?

PHILOXENUS [*clutching Bacchis II*]: Madly.

NICOBULUS: You disgusting old fool! You dare to fall in love at your age?

PHILOXENUS: Why not?

NICOBULUS: Because it's disgraceful!

PHILOXENUS: There, there. No need for talk like that. I'm not angry at my son, and you shouldn't be angry at yours. If they are in love, they're acting wisely.

BACCHIS I [*to Bacchis II, who has been watching all this in fascination*]: Now follow me.

NICOBULUS: Look! Here they come, those proven perpetrators of petty lace and persuasion. [*To Bacchis I*] Well then? Are you going to return our sons and my slave? or do you want me to use force?

[*Bacchis I embraces him*]

PHILOXENUS: Will you get away? You're certainly no gentleman addressing such a charming little girl with such uncharming words.

BACCHIS I [*to Nicobulus, as she makes advances*]: Oh, you nicest little old man in the whole wide world. About your naughty son's doings... don't fight it.

NICOBULUS [*still in her embrace*]: If you don't get away from me— why, no matter how pretty you are, I'll make you plenty sorry!

BACCHIS I: I can take it. I'm not one bit afraid of how hard you hit.

NICOBULUS [*aside*]: What a talker! Oh me, I'm the one that's afraid!

BACCHIS II [*to Bacchis I, with Philoxenus in her lap*]: This one is much more... how shall I say... at peace.

BACCHIS I [*to Nicobulus*]: Do come inside with me. If you want to, you can punish your son there.

NICOBULUS: Won't you keep away from me, you shameless creature?

BACCHIS I: Oh, you noble thing, do let me persuade you.

NICOBULUS: *You* persuade me?

BACCHIS II: *I* shall certainly persuade *this* one.

[*Passionately embraces Philoxenus*]

PHILOXENUS: I don't need any more persuading! Let's go inside!
BACCHIS II: Oh, you charming thing!
PHILOXENUS: What are the terms for going inside?
BACCHIS II: Being with me.
PHILOXENUS [*lyrical again*]
    You are . . . everything I've longed for . . .
NICOBULUS: I've seen worthless men in my time, but never have I
    seen one worth less than you.
PHILOXENUS [*agreeably*]: You're so right.
BACCHIS I [*to Nicobulus*]: Do come inside. There is lovely food, wine,
    perfumes . . .
NICOBULUS: Enough of your banquets! I don't care how much you
    entertain me! Chrysalus and my son have already tricked me
    out of four hundred gold pieces. I wouldn't pass up
    punishing that slave even if it costs another four hundred.
BACCHIS I: But if he gives you back half of the gold, will you come in
    then? And won't you pardon him?
PHILOXENUS: He'll do it.
NICOBULUS: I will *not*! I don't want to! I won't stand for it! Leave me
    alone. I prefer to make those two pay for this.
PHILOXENUS: So! You're as worthless as me! Try this moral on for
    size: "Those goods which the gods have given take heed you
    through your own fault do not lose." [*A wince of recognition
    from Nicobulus*] Here's half your gold back. Now go in, have a
    drink, go to bed.
NICOBULUS: *Me?* Drink in the same house where my own son is
    debauched?
PHILOXENUS: *You* need a drink!
NICOBULUS [*begins to slip*]: Well, come on, then. I'll force myself to
    do this, even though it's a disgrace to do it. You mean *I've* got
    to watch while she lies next to him on the couch?
BACCHIS I [*interposes*]: Oh no, dear! Quite the contrary! *I'll* be next
    to you. I'll make love to you and hold you in my arms.
NICOBULUS: Well, I *am* a little tense. I'm finished. I can scarcely
    keep on saying no.
BACCHIS I: Now, dear, even if you do enjoy yourself, this life we live
    is not at all a long one. What you've lost today will never come
    again once you're dead.
NICOBULUS [*desperately, to Philoxenus*]: What should I do?

PHILOXENUS: What should *you* do? At your age, you're asking that?

NICOBULUS: I want to. . .but I'm afraid to.

BACCHIS I: What are you afraid of?

NICOBULUS: Of humiliating myself in front of my son and my slave.

BACCHIS I: Honey baby, please dear, even if that happens, he *is*
your son. How do you think he's going to pay for everything
without your help? Oh, please do forgive them!

[*Kisses him*]

NICOBULUS [*aside*]:   How she drills through me! Has she convinced
me to do what I had sworn I would not? [*To Bacchis I*] Very
well, thanks to you and your hard work, I'm a scoundrel.

BACCHIS I [*aside*]:   How I wish it had been anyone's hard work but
mine! [*To Nicobulus*] Do I have your guarantee now?

NICOBULUS: Once I've said something, I never change.

BACCHIS I [*to both Nicobulus and Philoxenus*]:   The day is almost gone.
Both of you, go inside, lie down. Your sons are waiting for
you there.

NICOBULUS [*bitterly*]:   Yes, waiting for us to die, I would expect.

BACCHIS I: It's evening now. Follow me.

NICOBULUS: Lead us where you please. Just pretend we're your
slaves.

[*Nicobulus and Philoxenus start to go into Bacchis I's house*]

BACCHIS I [*to audience*]:   Two men who tried to trap their sons are
themselves trapped, victims of our charming plot.

[*Entire company enters*]

THE COMPANY

If these two old men had not been worthless
since boyhood, they'd not be snared in scandals
today in their hoary manhood; nor would we
much delight in our play's long survival,
had we not often seen pimps made rich
by greedy sons and fathers playing rivals!

Spectators all, farewell, we wish you well!
What you wish for us, your applause will tell.

[*Exeunt*]

NOTES

This translation is based for the most part on Cesare Questa, ed., *Titus Maccius Plautus: Bacchides* (Florence, 1975).

INTRODUCTION: THE PRODUCERS

1. With *Inferno*, canto 3.9, cf. *Bacchides* 368–70: "pandite atque aperite propere *ianuam hanc Orci* obsecro. / nam equidem haud aliter esse duco, quippe qui *nemo advenit, / nisi quem spes reliquere omnes* esse ut frugi possiet." The other famous line in the play is Chrysalus's quotation in IV.7 of an aphorism attributed first to Menander: ὃν οἱ θεοὶ φιλοῦσιν ἀποθνήσκει νέος, *quem di diligunt adulescens moritur*: "He whom the gods love dies young."

2. See E. W. Handley, *Menander and Plautus: A Study in Comparison* (London, 1968).

3. For Plautus's transformation of Menander see the notes to the translation of III.3–III.6.

4. On *Bacchides* I.1.A (the reconstructed opening scene) see n. 1 to the translation, below.

5. There are abusive terms in Latin for the profession of Bacchis I and II, and such words are sometimes used by angry male characters; e.g., *scortum* (literally, "hide"), which I generally render as *whore* or *slut*, and *illecebra* (literally, "allurement"), which comes across nicely as *hooker*. But Plautus's regular word for the sisters Bacchis is *meretrix*, which can be translated variously as a "woman earning wages" (cf. *merere*, "to earn money," "to draw pay"), "kept woman," and, as it is usually rendered here, "courtesan." In contemporary usage *courtesan* may seem too genteel compared with *prostitute*, *harlot*, or *whore*, but in most instances those words would serve as a harsh and misleading description of what the *meretrix* does. She is not coarse enough to be called a harlot, nor does she conduct her business in the streets, like a prostitute. Occasionally the context permits the translation "whore," but in most instances that word brings with it too heavy a charge of immorality. The *meretrix* is as much geisha as kept woman, and *courtesan* is the word that comes closest to conveying what coolly calculating characters Bacchis I and II really are.

6. This is also true of Phronesium and her lovers in *Truculentus* (see *Truculentus* I.1–II.1 and IV.4).

7. *Bacchides* is customarily dated prior to 191 B.C., at some date earlier than *Casina* and *Truculentus*. For the slave-playwright Pseudolus see John Wright, "The Transformations of Pseudolus," *Transactions and Proceedings of the American Philological Association* 105 (1975): 403–16.

BACCHIDES

1. The continuous text of *Bacchides* starts in the middle of a conversation between Bacchis of Athens and her sister Bacchis from Samos (I.1.B). Exactly how much has been lost before this point remains a difficult problem for which no conclusive answer seems possible. Some twenty fragments of the opening scene have been preserved and are conveniently arranged in the Loeb edition with Paul Nixon's translation (*Plautus* I.330–33). Attempts to reconstruct an opening of the play began in the Renaissance. In Angelius's edition of 1514, for example, a prologue spoken by the god Silenus is followed by an opening scene with Pistoclerus and his tutor Lydus. Friederich Leo outlined a more detailed (and dramatically more sensible) scenario. (The present version follows the plot he constructed from the fragments.) Pistoclerus tells of a letter he has received from his friend Mnesilochus at Ephesus in which

Mnesilochus reveals his infatuation for Bacchis, the sister of Pistoclerus's own mistress, Bacchis of Athens. Bacchis from Samos (or Bacchis II in the present script) is hired out to a soldier named Cleomachus for a year, and Mnesilochus hopes that Pistoclerus will find the two when they arrive in Athens and obtain her release. A slave of Bacchis runs in from the harbor with the news that Bacchis II has arrived. Bacchis II enters in the company of a boy who is a servant of Cleomachus. Both sisters meet Pistoclerus and decide to enlist his aid in freeing Bacchis II from her contract with the soldier. Others have added details to what Leo first outlined: a "delayed prologue" for Pistoclerus, in the style of *Miles Gloriosus*, and possibly a *canticum* for Cleomachus's boy. The recent discovery of the first line of Menander's *The Double Deceiver* (πρὸς τῶν θεῶν μειράκιον, "By the gods, young man") shows that his play opened with one of the sisters talking to Moschus (Pistoclerus). Unfortunately, there is no parallel in Plautus's play for the Greek line.

The present version (I.1.A) was composed by working backwards from the completed translation of the rest of the script. Bacchis I, Bacchis II, and Pistoclerus have the same diction and character as elsewhere. Bacchis I is the dominant sister, as she is in the final scene, and Pistoclerus is the earnest but not too bright youth we see later in the play. The opening scene is here made into a "mirror scene" of the finale (V.2), so that the two scenes frame the action of the inner play, the two plots that Chrysalus invents to help his young master Pistoclerus and his friend Mnesilochus. The opening scene is also roughly the same length as the finale. Rather than compose a formal prologue (or even a "delayed" one), I have made Pistoclerus talk about his friend Mnesilochus from a letter he has just received. This invention anticipates a motif used several times later in the play, where letters acquire a crucial role in the intrigues of Chrysalus (IV.4 and IV.9).

In all other respects this opening to *Bacchides* is a free invention based on most but not all of the fragments, and not necessarily in the order proposed by Leo and others. The result is an opening scene without prologue, *cantica*, or other ambitious theatrical effects, and one considerably shorter than the hundreds of lines which some scholars have proposed. It seemed to me that the longer such a confection grew, the more obvious it would become that the audience was watching something more exegetical than Plautine. I also thought it fair to signal to readers or audiences the moment at which genuine Plautus begins. The point is to free him of the responsibility of the opening scene, and also to make a joke. For that is what the lost and found opening of the *Bacchides* must be: a joke for the theater, not a recital of facts from a libretto.

2. This is the first of many times that Pistoclerus and others refer to Mnesilochus as his "old pal" (*sodalis*): the words appear over and over again on the lips of Pistoclerus and Lydus, and with increasing irony.

3. As the two sisters turn back to their conversation with Pistoclerus, they speak an elegant little jingle (their lines end respectively in *oratio . . . cantio*).

4. Literally, Lydus speaks of Lycurgus, the legendary founder of Sparta's constitution, who was famous for his incorruptibility.

5. This outrageous Plautine goddess named Suavisaviatio (literally, "amorous-kissing") is a confection of the verb *savior* (kiss) and adjective *suavis* (sweet). *Smoochabella* may be accompanied by at least one smack of the actor's lips.

6. Here and at other points a character's lines may be set off in quotation marks; for example, Chrysalus's famous lines in IV.7:

> "He whom the gods love dies young,
> while he still has his strength, sense, and wit."

The quotation marks are meant to underscore the artificiality and often the absurdity of the aphorisms which Plautus gives his characters to speak. Windy moralizing is a peculiarly male disease in this play. Lydus is the worst (or best) offender, but the contagion spreads to his pupil Pistoclerus, who in many ways is a younger version of his master. Pistoclerus's "old pal" Mnesilochus and the two fathers Nicobulus and Philoxenus also indulge in this habit. All of them are filled with well-worn advice and wise sayings, and none of this "wisdom" has the slightest effect on the course of events—except possibly to heighten the dramatic irony implicit in the actors' talking one way and acting another.

7. Lydus's name sounds very much like the word *ludus* (game, jest), the related verb *ludificari* (to make sport of, to fool), and *Lydus* (Lydian). Plautus plays with all of the homonyms in this scene.

8. This speech by Pistoclerus and the next speech by Lydus provide a modest display of Greek culture: Hercules killed his music teacher Linus in a sudden quarrel. Phoenix is the aged teacher of Achilles whose good advice the hero does not heed in *Iliad* 9.

9. Changed from the original. Strictly translated, Chrysalus says, "Although I love the *Epidicus* [a comedy by Plautus] like my own self, there's no play I so hate to see, if Pellio [Publilius Pellio, an actor contemporary with Plautus] is acting in it."

10. Chrysalus's name is close in sound to Croesus and the Greek *chrysos* (gold); in II.3, it inspires the comic word *Crucisalus* (cf. Latin *crux*, "cross"), "Crossalus" (Nixon's inspired invention).

11. Throughout this tale about the villainous Greek Archidemides, Chrysalus is obviously improvising as he goes, only one line ahead of Nicobulus.

12. Literally, ". . . to a bigger thief than Autolycus." Autolycus, grandfather of Odysseus, surpassed all men in theft and trickery.

13. Note that the ship of Chrysalus's fantastic story has now become an appropriate image for the distracted Nicobulus.

14. Lydus once again speaks in paratragic style. In this scene and in III.3, the audience begins to realize who is responsible for the moral diction of Pistoclerus.

15. The entrance of the bland Mnesilochus is in abrupt contrast to the high moral tone of Lydus.

16. This scene and the following are those parts of the play for which we have fragments from Menander's *The Double Deceiver*. Comparison shows that Plautus changed the names of the young men from the relatively simple Moschos and Sostratos to the more exotic Pistoclerus and Mnesilochus, and that of the clever slave Syros to Chrysalus (for its potential for wordplay). Lydus remains Lydus, again for the sake of puns. Mnesilochus's monologue is twice as long as the speech of Sostratos (Mnesilochus) in Menander, and all the business about begging his father to forgive Chrysalus is not in Menander at all.

17. These lines of misunderstanding between the two friends are not in Menander; they were added by Plautus for their heavy dramatic irony.

18. In the original, there is very possibly an allusion here to Menander's *Dis Exapaton*: "I have no use for those Parmenos and Syruses. . . ." Syrus is the name of the slave whose role Chrysalus assumes in Plautus.

19. Mnesilochus's lines are the key to understanding Chrysalus's fantastically complex lies in the second plot which he invents for Nicobulus. The way to deceive the old man now will be to say only what would seem to *harm* Chrysalus; although Nicobulus will believe the opposite is the truth, he will in fact be duped into *helping* Chrysalus.

20. In the Greek myth, Bellerophon carried a sealed letter which contained instructions for his own execution.

21. Chrysalus's line is a typical explosion of alliteration: *pacisci cum illo paullula pecunia / potes* (lines 865–66).

22. The less familiar deities in Chrysalus's oath are Spes (Hope), Opis (Plenty), Virtus (Virtue), and Summanus (an obscure god of lightning and thunderbolts).

23. In the original there is an allusion to characters in a once-familiar comedy: ". . . more hard words from me than Clinia heard from Demetrius."

24. Textual critics have objected to much of Chrysalus's "Song of Troy" because he seems to be slipping from one role to another. At first he laments for Priam, as though sympathetic to the Trojans; then he shifts to the role of a boastful Greek. Strenuous efforts have been made to arrive at a single, "Trojan" or "Greek" voice for the *canticum* by removing any lines that contradict a single message. This is to suppose, of course, that Plautus intended for Chrysalus's solo to be a coherent, logical exposition of the fall of Nicobulus as the fall of Troy. The present version incorporates all (or very nearly all) of the lines assigned to Chrysalus, because I do not believe that Chrysalus is attempting to give a tidy lecture, but rather that he is trying to play at the high style of epic and tragedy, shifting now to this theme, now to that; hence in this version the actor is asked alternately to declaim bad Milton, bad national anthem, and boring lecture notes. The scene carries very nicely if it is played by a number of *personae*, not just one. Chrysalus's lines are funny precisely because they are such a hodgepodge of little learning about the famous names associated with the fall of Troy.

25. Another jingle: *exitium, excidium, exlecebra fiet hic equos hodie auro senis* (line 944).

26. Literally, Chrysalus refers to the Palladium, a sacred image of Athena kept in the citadel of Troy. It was believed that the city's survival depended on its safe custody. Diomedes and Odysseus carried it off to ensure the fall of Troy.

27. "General" Chrysalus ends his report on the campaign against Nicobulus by slipping into the absolute constructions typical of official Roman documents: *salute nostra atque urbe capta per dolum / domum redduco iam integrum omnem exercitum* (lines 1070–71).

28. The sisters reappear at the precise moment when all of Chrysalus's plotting has run its full course.

29. Philoxenus's romantic language (*cor stimulo foditur*) is turned to obscenity by Nicobulus's substitution of the target of Love's piercing (*pol tibi multo aequius est coxen dicem* [line 1159]).

CASINA or
THE LOT-DRAWERS

LUST IN ACTION

The older Plautus got, some scholars think, the fonder he became of writing *cantica*. Since *Casina* has more *cantica* than any other of Plautus's works, it has been dated to 185 B.C., no more than a year or so before the playwright's presumed death in 184 / 183 B.C. One passage in the play offers more substantial evidence for a late date. When the plotting of the lecherous old man Lysidamus is exposed, he attempts to weasel out of the situation by blaming his conduct on Bacchantes, women in an ecstatic Dionysiac orgy. This ploy is immediately checked by his neighbor's wife, Myrrhina:

> He's making that up!
> Everyone knows the Bacchic orgies
> aren't playing here now. (V.4)

This is perhaps an allusion to the worship of Dionysus at Rome, which was the subject of a decree by the senate in 186 B.C. (the *Senatus Consultum de Bacchanalibus*).

Casina is based on Diphilus's *Kleroumenoi*, or *The Lot-Drawers*, produced between 332 B.C. and 320 B.C. Only the title of Diphilus's play survives. The prologue of *Casina* says that Plautus called his play *Sortientes*, the Latin translation of Diphilus's Greek title, and it has been suggested that the title *Casina* dates only from the revival after Plautus's death.[1] But *Casina* is an appropriate title for the play we have because it is the characters' obsession either to save her or to ruin her that supplies all the energies of the drama.

Casina is a story of romance and hidden identities, with comic peripety and recognition scenes forming the climax of the work. As is often the case, the play focuses only on the interesting consequences of earlier, less interesting actions. Many years before, a young girl (Casina) had been abandoned on the doorstep of Lysidamus and his wife Cleostrata. She was raised as a servant to the mistress of the household. Lysidamus's young son Euthynicus fell in love with her and hoped to marry her. But as the wedding drew near, Lysidamus wanted her for himself, and he contrived a fantastic plot in which he first sent Euthynicus off to the country and then arranged for his overseer Olympio to marry her instead. It is at this point that *Casina* opens. Lysidamus's wife Cleostrata opposes him with her slave Chalinus, who serves as a stand-in for Euthynicus. What begins as a conflict between father and son thus turns into a struggle between wife and husband, with slaves as the surrogate actors for the opposing parties. Cleostrata attempts to resolve the conflict by drawing lots with her husband. Unfortunately, Lysidamus wins. She and her servants then invent one scheme after another to cheat Lysidamus of his prize. After a thorough beating and public disclosure of all his sins, Lysidamus is at last reunited with his wife and their household more or less returns to normal. A brief epilogue tells us that Casina is in reality a free-born Athenian who will soon marry her former master Euthynicus.

Those who prefer Greek New Comedy to Roman have sometimes claimed that the Roman playwrights vulgarized their Greek models, coarsening what were originally refined and delicate comedies of manners to please the grosser tastes of the Roman audiences on which they depended for their livelihood.[2] But this Hellenic view of Roman comedy may not be correct. Many of the spectacular scenes of *Casina* have their parallels in Aristophanes (and probably also in the lost poets of Middle Comedy): homosexuality and transvestism (*The Women of the Thesmophoria*), denial of sex and war between the sexes (*Lysistrata*), and parodies of marriage ceremonies and wedding hymns (*Birds, Peace*). The bawdy episodes of *Casina* need by no means be attributed to Plautus's desire to pitch his comedy at a lower, "Roman" level. Diphilus's own play may have been, not a refined comedy of romance and recognition, but one of conflict between members of the family, between the generations, between husband and wife, and the slaves who represent them. More to the point, the farcical scenes of *Casina* are not simply Plautus's way of playing to the pit; they are episodes integral to the basic themes of the play. The romance and recognition of Casina's true identity are only given passing mention in the prologue and epilogue. The heart of the play we have is a comic *agon*, or contest, between Lysidamus and forces protecting his son Euthynicus.

Although *Casina* is played by the usual repertory of the stock characters in New Comedy, the personality of Lysidamus is the key to the play's action. The rest of the players react to his character; indeed they exist as characters chiefly in reaction to him. The spectacular comic scenes of the play are spectacular responses to Lysidamus: the lot drawing (II.6), Pardalisca's mad scene (III.5), the mock wedding (IV.4), and Olympio's "messenger speech" (V.2). Lysidamus acts in complete reversal of the roles he ought to be playing as husband, father, and master of his own house. His sexual aggression is pervasive and indiscriminate, directed against not only Casina but his male slaves as well (II.8). He is an *amator*, but a *senex amator*: not simply the lover, but the old man as lover, and as slave to his passions he becomes a slave to his slave Olympio and then a slave to everyone he should master but cannot (III.8). He confuses social roles, and he also confuses sexuality. His desires give rise to a plot in which male identity is masked with female identity, as his sexual aggression is turned against him by the women of his house.[3]

Lysidamus's sexual fantasies, gluttony, and total abdication of the customary role of father, husband, and head of his household create an extraordinary pattern of images. The lot-drawing scene is a military encounter between the two parts of a household which should be joined together (II.6). Food is equated with sexual appetite, so that fish and other kinds of delicacies are mixed up in his imagination with his sexual appetite for Casina (II.8, III.6). The spice and fragrance of women, symbolized by such names as Casina (cinnamon) and Myrrhina (myrrh), find a counterimage in the stench of Lysidamus's body and his breath. He seeks to disguise himself with perfume, only to be repulsed first by his wife and then by his accomplice-slave Olympio (II.3, III.6). Sexual and gastronomic imagery become as one in Olympio's "messenger speech" about his wedding night with Casina, in which he tells of the "sword" he discovered in bed with his bride (V.2). The fantasy of the play is outrageous, but there is a logic to even the most frenzied scenes. Plautus's parody of tragedy is particularly well conceived. The mock wedding and nuptial couch of the male "Casina" are perversions of a real wedding, in response to Lysidamus's intended perversions

(IV.4). In her "mad scene" (III.5), Pardalisca describes a deranged Casina running about the house with a sword to slay her husband. Later, the long "messenger speech" of Olympio begins with his account of his search for that tragic heroine's sword and ends with his discovery of Chalinus's "sword" (V.2). But the sword that he grips is the phallus. The symbol of male dominance of the female brings about the complete overthrow of the male and becomes merely the phallus of comedy, an object of ridicule, not power.

It would seem that Lysidamus is very much the villain of the piece. Some critics have gone so far as to suggest that Cleostrata is one of the most morally attractive women in all of Plautus. She is busily defending her rights, as well as the rights of her son, and if romantic love were more central to the play this would be a reasonable interpretation of the character of Lysidamus and Cleostrata. But Plautus pushes the "barrier comedy" of thwarted young lovers completely out of his play. The obsessions of Lysidamus and the contests they inspire become the central theme. *Casina* thereby leads us to something more complicated than a restoration of Lysidamus and Cleostrata to their customary roles of husband, father, wife, and mother.

The opening lines of the two antagonists reveal much about their characters. Cleostrata is all sternness and imperatives:

> *Lock* the doors to the pantry and *bring* the keys to me.

By contrast, Lysidamus is never in touch with the realities of a world for which he is responsible. He enters from the first lost in a lover's fantasy:

> I believe that love
> surpasses everything,
> the gleaming stars.

The play can create powerful tensions in the sympathies of its audience. It is not insignificant that the husband and wife are more than once likened to Jupiter and Juno, that divine pair locked forever in resentful middle age (II.3 and II.6). On the one hand, we know that Lysidamus (Jupiter) is dead wrong and bound to be punished; on the other hand, the implacable Cleostrata (Juno) and her accomplices go so far in their humiliation of Lysidamus that an audience will find itself coming to a more sympathetic reaction to him than perhaps it expected. The effect in performance is that in laughing at Lysidamus we come to feel a wry affection for him, even though we know that Cleostrata is upholding stern Roman (or Greek) virtues by her actions. In short, Cleostrata enjoys her anger and her stern morality, but Lysidamus has much more fun. The contrivances of Cleostrata, Pardalisca, and Chalinus are brilliant, and Olympio and Lysidamus are made complete fools; but those inventions and brilliant scenes are created in the first instance because of the obsessions of Lysidamus. His character creates the world of the drama, which, with a remarkable economy of invention and imagery, exists entirely in response to him.

In *Casina* we have not only a brilliant farce but the earliest version of a tale which Machiavelli much admired and adapted in *La Clizia* (1494). *Casina* also foreshadows the plot of Beaumarchais' *Le Marriage de Figaro* and thus, at still further remove, the collaboration of Mozart and Da Ponte in *Le Nozze di Figaro*.

CASINA or
THE LOT-DRAWERS

CHARACTERS

PROLOGUE
OLYMPIO, *slave and overseer of Lysidamus*
CHALINUS, *slave ally of Cleostrata*
CLEOSTRATA, *wife of Lysidamus*
PARDALISCA, *servant and maid of Cleostrata*
MYRRHINA, *wife of Alcesimus, friend of Cleostrata*
LYSIDAMUS, *old man, husband of Cleostrata*
ALCESIMUS, *old man, husband of Myrrhina*
CITRIO, *cook*
Attendants to Olympio, Cleostrata, Pardalisca, and Citrio

[*Scene: A street in Athens with the houses of Alcesimus and Lysidamus*]

PROLOGUE
Kind greetings to all gathered in this place,
beloved of Fides, sharing Fides' grace!
My truthful words deserve like courtesy:
applause will show how fair you are to me.

[*Bows and continues*]

[Your drinker of a vintage wine is wise,
as also he who ancient plays does prize—
the plays of Classical antiquity,

well made for today's gross iniquity,
with shows appearing daily thick and fast,
like coins, each issue worth less than the last.
And then there's the message many brought us:
"We'd like to see another show by Plautus!"
Perhaps one or two will know this play?
No Romans here, eh? Then I'm bound to say,
since only works of merit should survive,
that none deserves more than this to be revived.
So far did our flower of poets surpass the rest
that from the first this one was judged his best.
Poet may fallen be, not to rise again;
yet what he wrote can teach, if not the man.
So set your minds with ours in harmony
and learn the purpose of our company.][1]

No doubts or debts need any fear today,
no chance you'll get in bill collector's way.
Enjoy your games, from every debt be free:
it's Siesta-fiesta officially![2]
Now, your tellers only check accounts, not funds;
there'll be time enough tomorrow for their duns.
So listen and forget all business claims;
it's time to give our comedy some names.
Kleroumenoi and later *Sortientes*[3]
were titles fit for ancient audiences
of Greeks and Romans—hardly your condition—
say *The Lot-Drawers*, or *They Used Sortition*.
To Athens Greek Diphilus first brought it,
then Plautus wrote it out again, for plaudits.[4]

[*Points to the house of Lysidamus*]

Here dwells an old married man with spouse.
Their only son lives with them in the house.
He counts among his slaves a certain valet,
a fellow sick today upon his pallet.
That slave some sixteen years ago and more
one morning saw a foundling at their door,
a baby just left there by her mother.
He asked her, could he take it to another?

No sooner was her quick consent made known
than home he flew; would mistress like to own
the child? She would. She raised her up so well
the true maternity no one could tell.
This girl has reached an age where she can vex
with charms the members of the other sex
and throw her household into passion's throes.
The father and his son are hard opposed
to one another; legions both prepare,
and both assume the other's unaware.
The father first acquired his overseer's aid,
a slave to pose as bridegroom to the maid.
The son then got his carrier of arms
to be his proxy, to enjoy her charms,
to marry her and serve in master's stead;
she then could transfer to her master's bed.
But when his wife got wind of all this fun
she promptly joined up forces with her son.
Then, to change his son's erotic focus
the father found him an exotic locus;
without that filial impediment
he now expects his love life's betterment.
The son will still prevail: though absentee,
he profits from a mother's loyalty.
But don't expect the boy to come today.
Plautus put a roadblock in his way.

I'm sure there are those here who shake their heads
and ask, "What's this? You say that *slaves* can wed?
A courtship and a marriage you propose?
You're showing things no other nation knows!"
Well, I assure you, in more southern climes
such ceremonies happen all the time:
among the Greeks and all peoples Punic,
and Apulians, who wear our Roman tunic.[5]
You know, it's *there* they take such pains to see
more weddings for the slave than for the free!
If any doubt this is the way things are,
I'll wager honeyed wine, a brimming jar—
provided judge be Carthaginians,

oh-so-trusty Greeks, or faithful Apulians.
What's your pleasure? Does no one have a thirst?
I thought so. Back to her I spoke of first,
the maid whose good these plotting knaves so scorn.
She'll be revealed a virgin, and free-born,
a citizen of Athens, as you'll see,
untouched by all our play's iniquity.
Then, once our show is over—for a fee,
of course—I absolutely guarantee
that any man may have her at his side
without the costly rituals due a bride.

[*Turns to go; pauses*]

In war, succeed; in business deals, excel!
With these last words your Prologue says, "Farewell."

[*Bows; exit*]

I.1

[*The country slave Olympio stalks out of the house of Lysidamus, followed closely by the city slave Chalinus*]

OLYMPIO

So you're not going to let me alone, are you?
So I can't speak or think unless I have your say-so?
Why the devil do you keep following me around?

CHALINUS

Because I've decided to follow you all the time,
everywhere you go, just like your shadow.
If you wanted to go to hell, I'd be right behind you!
Now you, with your clever scheming tricks, just try to snatch
Casina for your bride! I know you want to.

OLYMPIO

What's it to you?

CHALINUS

What's it to me, you shameless wretch?
What's an underhanded overseer like you
doing slinking into town?

OLYMPIO

I like to come to town.

CHALINUS

Why aren't you off in the country in your own province?
Why don't you mind the office you're supposed
to mind and keep yourself out of city affairs?
You've come here to snatch *my* bride away.
Go back to the country now! Back to your own province!

OLYMPIO

Chalinus, I haven't forgotten my duties.
I left someone well in charge of things in the country.
If I get what I came to town for,
to marry the woman you're dying to have,
that pretty little Casina, your fellow slave,
I'll lead her off with me as my bride to the country
and then I'll be secure enough *in the country*,

[*Snarling*]

in my own province.

CHALINUS: You're going to marry *her*? By Hercules, I'd rather hang
myself than let you have her!

OLYMPIO: She's already my catch. Go ahead, stick your head in a
noose.

CHALINUS: You summit of a dungheap! She's *your* catch?

OLYMPIO: You'll see soon enough.

CHALINUS: Damn you!

OLYMPIO: Just think of all the ways you'll suffer on my wedding
day!

CHALINUS: What will you do to me?

OLYMPIO

What will I do to you?
First, you'll hold the wedding torch for my new bride.
Then you'll be a worthless good-for-nothing.[6]
Next, whenever you come to our farmhouse,
you'll get *one* jug, *one* path, *one* spring,
one copper pail, and *eight* vats to fill!
AND if they aren't filled with water all the time,
my whip will give you blisters that will be!

[*Yanks Chalinus's head down by the hair*]

I'll bend you so from carrying water

you'll be able to serve as a horse's crupper.
After that—IN THE COUNTRY—you might eat a heap of hay,
you might eat a pile of earth like an earthworm,
but if you ask for anything else,
Hunger herself won't be as hungry
as I'll make you, IN THE COUNTRY!
After that, when you're worn out,
famished with hunger,
I'll see you sleep the way you deserve to.

CHALINUS: And how will you do that?

OLYMPIO: You'll be squeezed up tight in the window where you can
curse when I kiss her, when she says to me,

[In a squeaky voice]

"My soul-a-wollie, my Olympio,
my life, my honey-bunny, my holiday,
let me kiss your iddy-biddy eyes, my joy,
my little sparrow, my cooing dove, my RABBIT!"
While she says all this to me, you—villain—
why, you'll scamper around like a mouse inside a wall.
Now don't try to answer me. I'm going inside.
Talking with you is such a bore!

[Stalks back into the house of Lysidamus]

CHALINUS: I'm coming after you, Olympio! I'll be damned if you do
anything here without my knowing it.

[Follows after him]

II.1

[Enter Cleostrata and Pardalisca from the house of Lysidamus]

CLEOSTRATA [sternly, to slaves inside the house]:   Lock the doors to the
pantry and bring the keys to me. I'm going next-door to the
neighbors'. If my husband wants me for anything, you can
reach me there.

PARDALISCA: The old man has ordered a meal to be fixed for him.

CLEOSTRATA: Hush! Keep quiet! Go inside! There won't be any
cooking here today.

[Pardalisca goes back inside]

Since he's working against me
and his own son to gratify *only* his desires,
I'LL PAY HIM BACK WITH HUNGER,
I'LL PAY HIM BACK WITH THIRST,
WITH MALEDICTIONS
WITH MALEFACTIONS
I'LL FIX THAT LOVERBOY.

[*Sweetly*]

I'll torment him with language he won't like.

[*Resumes her tirade*]

I'll see to it that he lives the life he deserves:
THAT HAYSTACK FROM HADES!
THAT CHASER AFTER CHASTITY!
THAT STABLE OF SCANDALS!

[*Calms herself; rearranges her clothing, fusses with her hair*]

Now I'll go next-door and complain about my bad luck.

[*Door to Alcesimus's house opens*]

But the door is opening! The very person I'm looking for is
coming out. I don't think I left home soon enough.

II.2

MYRRHINA [*entering from house of Alcesimus, to servants inside*]: You women follow me. We're going next-door. You in there! Does anyone hear what I'm saying? I'll be next-door if my husband or anyone else asks for me.

[*To audience, cheerfully*]

When I'm at home by myself, I find it hard to work.

[*To servants again*]

Didn't I tell you to bring me my weaving?

CLEOSTRATA: Why, Myrrhina, hello.

MYRRHINA: Hello indeed. But tell me, why are you looking so sad?

CLEOSTRATA: It's the way women usually look who have a bad marriage. There's always plenty going wrong inside and outside the house. In fact, I was on my way to see you.

MYRRHINA: My goodness, I was just coming over to see you. But why are you so upset now? Whatever bothers you is just as much a bother to me.

CLEOSTRATA: And I *do* believe you. There's no neighbor I love more than you—and with good reason. I can't think of any other woman who has more of those good qualities I should like to have myself.

MYRRHINA: I'd like to know what's bothering you.

CLEOSTRATA: I'm treated like dirt in my own house.

MYRRHINA: Oh no! Why? *Please* tell me!

[*Aside*]

Especially since I don't understand what you're complaining about.

CLEOSTRATA: It's my husband! He treats me like dirt! I have lost the right to exercise my rights.

MYRRHINA [*puzzled*]:   That's amazing, if what you say is true. Generally it's men who don't get their rights from their wives.

CLEOSTRATA: Nevertheless, against my will he's asked for my little serving girl—the one who belongs to me—the one I brought up at my own expense to give to his overseer. But he's in love with her himself!

MYRRHINA: Shh! Don't say another word!

[*Looks around apprehensively*]

CLEOSTRATA: But surely it's all right to talk now. We're alone.

MYRRHINA: [*runs about and looks carefully up and down street; returns in a calmer mood*]:   Why, so we are. Wherever did you get her? Surely it's not right for a decent woman to have private property behind her husband's back. Any woman who does has come by it either by stealing it from her husband or by selling herself on the street. It is my opinion that every single thing you own belongs to your husband.

CLEOSTRATA: And everything you've said was said against a friend!

MYRRHINA: Now, hush, you simpleton, and listen to me. Don't set yourself against him. Let him make love, let him do what he wants to, as long as you're well provided for at home.

CLEOSTRATA: Are you sure you're feeling well? What you're saying is clearly against your own best interests.

MYRRHINA: Silly! Always take care to avoid these words from your husband.

CLEOSTRATA: What words?

MYRRHINA [*in baritone*]:   "Wife, I divorce you."

CLEOSTRATA: Shh! Be quiet!

MYRRHINA: What is it?

CLEOSTRATA [*hears the sound of Lysidamus's singing offstage*]:   There!

MYRRHINA: Who is it? Who do you see?

CLEOSTRATA: It's my husband! Go inside! Please hurry!

MYRRHINA: I'll go, if that's what you want.

CLEOSTRATA: I'll have a free moment soon, and then I'll talk with you. Good-by for now.

MYRRHINA: Good-by.

[*Goes inside Alcesimus's house*]

II.3

[*Lysidamus enters singing*]

LYSIDAMUS

I believe that love
surpasses everything,
the gleaming stars.
You can't name me anything with
greater taste
or greater charm.
I simply have to marvel
at those cooks with all their spices,
they never seem to use
this one,
the best of all.
I believe when love's the spice
it's sure to please,
no doubt at all.
No dish can taste sweet or sour
if love's not there.
Whatever's rank and randy,
it makes a piece of candy,
it makes whatever's fell, swell,
a grouch can be all charm and grace.

[*Descends from lyric mode; confides to the audience*]

Nobody had to tell me this.
I learned it all myself, at home.
Now that I'm in love with Casina
I surpass in charm Charm herself.
I've gone around to all the perfume sellers.
Wherever there's a nice perfume,
I perfume, just to please her.
And I *do* please her, as I see it.
But my wife, because she's *alive*,
is a torture to me.

[*At last he sees Cleostrata*]

Look at her standing there, scowling. I'll have to greet this
bad piece of news in a mild-mannered way.[7]

[*Pauses; fixes his face in a smile*]

Oh my wife and my delight . . . what's up?

[*Tries to embrace her*]

CLEOSTRATA [*pushes him away*]: Go away! Take your hands off me!
LYSIDAMUS: Now, now, my Juno, it's not nice to be so mean to your
    Jupiter. Where are you going?
CLEOSTRATA: Leave me alone!
LYSIDAMUS: Stay here!
CLEOSTRATA: I'm not staying here!
LYSIDAMUS: Then I'll follow you!
CLEOSTRATA: Tell me, do you feel all right?
LYSIDAMUS: Certainly I feel all right. Oh, how I love you!

[*Holds her in a locking embrace*]

CLEOSTRATA: I don't want your love.
LYSIDAMUS: You won't get that wish.
CLEOSTRATA [*struggles to get free*]: You're killing me.
LYSIDAMUS [*aside*]: I wish you were telling the truth.
CLEOSTRATA [*overhears him; aside*]: I believe *that* well enough.
LYSIDAMUS: Now look this way, my sweet.
CLEOSTRATA: Yes, as sweet as you are to me.

[*Sniffs*]

Wherever did you get that perfume?

LYSIDAMUS [*aside, to audience*]:   I'm done for! I'm caught for sure, poor me! Why did I wait so long to wipe it off my head? May Mercury the god of commerce ruin you, you perfume seller! You sold me the stuff!

CLEOSTRATA: You scoundrel! You gray-headed, unnatural gnat! I can hardly keep from telling you what you ought to know. Old as you are, to walk through the streets, reeking with perfume. You old fool!

LYSIDAMUS: Actually I was just helping a friend of mine while he was buying the perfume.

CLEOSTRATA [*aside*]:   How quickly he made that one up!

[*To Lysidamus*]

Aren't you ashamed of yourself?

LYSIDAMUS: Say anything you want to about me.

CLEOSTRATA: What brothel have you been lying in now?

LYSIDAMUS: *Me?* In a brothel?

CLEOSTRATA: I know more than you think I do.

LYSIDAMUS: Well, then, what do you know?

CLEOSTRATA [*backs him down until he collapses into a heap on the floor*]:   Of all old men, there is no old man more worthless than you are. Where have you come from, you rascal? Where have you been? What whorehouse were you visiting? Where were you drinking? Ye gods, you're drunk! Look how wrinkled your cloak is!

LYSIDAMUS: May the gods curse both of us with bad luck if I put so much as one drop of wine in my mouth today!

CLEOSTRATA [*unimpressed*]:   Oh, by all means, do as you please. Drink, eat, squander our money.

LYSIDAMUS [*rising*]

Stop! That's enough for now, wife!

CONTROL YOURSELF!

YOU'RE GETTING A BIT SHRILL!

LEAVE YOURSELF SOMETHING TO NAG ME ABOUT TOMORROW!

[*In a milder tone*]

But tell me, now that you've calmed down, why don't you do what your husband asks you to do rather than fight him all the time?

CLEOSTRATA [*also in a milder tone*]:   Why, whatever do you have in mind?

LYSIDAMUS: You ask? I have the maid Casina in mind. I have in mind to marry her to our overseer, an honest slave who can supply her well with wood, hot water, food, dresses, one who can rear the *children* she will bear . . .

[*Looks off into space, imagining the begetting of children; comes to and resumes*]

a better slave than the one you'd give her to, an armorbearer and a scoundrel, a man who doesn't have a single coin in his purse.

CLEOSTRATA: How strange that at your age you don't remember your duty.

LYSIDAMUS: Why do you say that?

CLEOSTRATA: Because if you acted properly and decently, you would let me look after the maids. That's my concern.

LYSIDAMUS: Why the devil do you want to give her to a shieldcarrier?

CLEOSTRATA: Because we clearly must support our only son.

LYSIDAMUS: He may be *our* only son, but he's no more an only son to me than I'm an only father to him.

[*Cleostrata starts to reply but thinks better of it*]

He ought to yield to my desires rather than to his.

CLEOSTRATA: You're asking for trouble, my good man. [*Aside*] He's sniffed me out, I see.

LYSIDAMUS: *Me?*

CLEOSTRATA: You. Why else would you be babbling? What are you so eager for?

LYSIDAMUS: That she be given to an honest slave rather than to a wicked slave.

CLEOSTRATA: What if I beg and plead with our overseer Olympio to let Chalinus have her for *my* sake?

LYSIDAMUS: But what if I beg that weaponcarrier to let Olympio have her? I think he would grant that request.

CLEOSTRATA [*appears resigned*]:   Very well, then. Do you want me to call Chalinus outside for your instructions? You ask him, and I'll ask the overseer.

LYSIDAMUS: I'm game.

CLEOSTRATA: He's on his way. Now we'll find out which of us is more persuasive.

[*Goes into house*]

LYSIDAMUS: Now at last I can say it: may Hercules and all the gods ruin that woman! Ah, poor me, I'm tortured by love. She's opposing me on purpose. My wife has sniffed me out. That soldier-slave will have to be carefully watched in this affair. As for him! Would that all the gods and goddesses

[*Chalinus enters*]

ruin. . .

II.4

CHALINUS [*steps on Lysidamus's line*][8]: . . . YOU! Er, sir, your wife said that you called me.

LYSIDAMUS: Yes, I did indeed order you to be called.

CHALINUS [*in supremely bored tone*]: Tell me what you want done.

LYSIDAMUS: First of all, I want you to wipe that frown off your face! It's stupid for you to scowl at a person who packs a more powerful punch!

[*In a milder tone*]

I've thought for some time that you were a sensible and honest fellow.

CHALINUS: Yes, I know. If that's your opinion, then why not set me free?

LYSIDAMUS: I want to, indeed I do! But what I want done doesn't mean anything if you don't help by doing something too.

CHALINUS [*bored*]: I'd like to know what you would like done.

LYSIDAMUS: Listen, I'll tell you. I've promised to give Casina as a bride to our overseer.

CHALINUS: But your wife and son have promised her to me!

LYSIDAMUS: I know. But would you prefer to be a free bachelor now, or to live out your life with your children as a married slave? The choice is yours. Choose whichever terms you please.

CHALINUS: If I were a free man, I would live at my own expense. Now I live at yours. As far as Casina is concerned, I won't budge. She goes to no other man alive.

LYSIDAMUS [*loses patience*]: Go inside at once! Call my wife without delay. Bring out an urn with you, and water, and lots.

CHALINUS: All right.

LYSIDAMUS: By the gods, I'll parry this thrust of yours. If I can't get anything I want this way

[*Gestures threateningly with staff*]

at least I can draw a lot. That's how I'll fix you and your fellow *citizens*.

[*With a sneer*]

CHALINUS: You just wait. May I draw the winning lot...

LYSIDAMUS [*steps on Chalinus's line*]: ...so you can die by agonizing torture!

CHALINUS: She'll marry me. Go ahead and hatch as many plots as you please.

LYSIDAMUS: Aren't you out of my sight yet?

CHALINUS [*nonchalantly*]: Can't stand the sight of me, eh? Still I'm well enough off.

[*Saunters into house*]

LYSIDAMUS [*to audience*]: Am I a poor wretch or am I not? Isn't everything going against me? Now I'm afraid my wife will ask Olympio not to marry Casina. If that happens, I'm ruined. A worthless old man. If she doesn't get her way, there's still a teensy bit of hope in the lot-drawing. But if *that* last chance trickles away,

[*In tragic style, à la Ajax*]

Why ... then ...
my sword shall be made my bed
and upon it shall I lie.

[*Collapses in a heap; enter Olympio from the house*]

But look! How nice! Here's Olympio.

[*Springs up*]

II.5

OLYMPIO [*speaks loudly to Cleostrata within so that Lysidamus will hear*]: You may as well put me in a hot oven and bake me until I'm brown as a biscuit, ma'am, as get what you want from me!

LYSIDAMUS [*aside*]:   I'm saved! My hopes are saved, to judge from these words!

OLYMPIO [*continues to yell to Cleostrata inside*]:   Why are you threatening me, ma'am, with your talk of freedom? Even if you and your son don't want to give it to me, even with both of you against me and totally opposed, I can become free for a very small fee.

LYSIDAMUS: What are you saying? Who are you fighting with now, Olympio?

OLYMPIO: The same woman you're always fighting with.

LYSIDAMUS: Oh, you mean my wife?

OLYMPIO: What do you mean, "my wife"?

[*Confidentially*]

You're like a hunter, you know. You spend your days and nights with a bitch.

LYSIDAMUS: What is she up to? What did she say to you?

OLYMPIO: She asks me—no, she *begs* me—not to marry Casina.

LYSIDAMUS: What did you say to her then?

OLYMPIO: I swore that I wouldn't give Casina away to Jupiter himself if he asked me.[9]

LYSIDAMUS: May the gods bless you for that!

OLYMPIO: Now she's all in a ferment, swollen up at me.

LYSIDAMUS: Gods, I wish she'd split right down the middle!

OLYMPIO: Gods, I believe she already did, if you're worth your salt as a husband!

[*Laughs at his own wit; Lysidamus winces*]

But—gods—your love *life* will be the *death* of me! Your wife hates me, your son hates me, the other slaves hate me . . .

LYSIDAMUS: What's any of that to you? As long as Jupiter here is on your side, these lesser gods won't amount to a fluff of flax.

OLYMPIO: Now that's a lot of nonsense! As if you didn't know how suddenly a mortal Jupiter can die! But when you're finally a *dead* Jupiter, when your kingdom has been turned over to the lesser gods, who will come to the aid of my back, my legs, or my head?

LYSIDAMUS: Your affairs are in better shape than you think *if* we succeed in seeing to it that I sleep with Casina.

OLYMPIO: I don't think that will ever happen. Your wife is dead set against giving her to me.

LYSIDAMUS: But this is what I'll do. I'll cast the lots into the urn and draw for you and Chalinus. I know where things stand now! We'll have to draw our swords and fight it out.

OLYMPIO: But what if the lot turns out the way you don't want it to?

LYSIDAMUS [*religiously*]: Don't be blasphemous! I trust in the gods. We'll put our faith in the lap of the gods.

[*Stares off into the heavens; Olympio surveys him up and down incredulously*]

OLYMPIO: I wouldn't buy what you've just said for a fiddle-dee-diddley-dee. *All* mortal men put their trust in the gods, but I still see many who put their trust in the gods deceived in the end.

LYSIDAMUS: Shh! Keep quiet.

OLYMPIO: What is it?

LYSIDAMUS: Look!

[*Points to house*]

Chalinus is coming out of our house with an urn and lots. Now we'll join battle with all our banners raised on high!

[*Lysidamus, Olympio, and servants march as if in formation; they take up position on one side of the stage*]

II.6

[*Enter Chalinus, Cleostrata, and the other servants with urn, water, and lots; they march into formation on the opposite side of the stage*]

CLEOSTRATA [*in stiff, soldierly style*]: Tell me, Chalinus, what is it my husband wants me to do?

CHALINUS: I believe he wants to see you dead and burning outside the city gate.

CLEOSTRATA: I believe that *is* what he wants.

CHALINUS: I don't believe it at all. I know it for certain.

LYSIDAMUS [*overhearing the exchange*]: There's more cunning here than I thought. I seem to have a soothsayer in the house. Let's lift our banners on high and go forth to oppose them. Follow me.

[*Marches up to Chalinus and Cleostrata*]

What are you doing here?

CHALINUS: Everything you asked for is here: wife, lots, water, and me.

OLYMPIO [*breaks in*]: With *you* here there's one thing more than I want.

CHALINUS: It well may seem that way to you. I'll sting you now, I'll pierce your little heart, you whipping post. You're already scared and sweaty.

LYSIDAMUS: Shut up, Chalinus.

CHALINUS: Take this fellow in hand!

OLYMPIO: No, you take *him* in hand! He's *used* to being taken in hand!

LYSIDAMUS [*getting things back under control*]: Bring the urn here. Give me the lots. Pay attention now.

[*Wheedling, to Cleostrata*]

I thought that you would see your way to granting me this favor, wife of mine, that Casina be married to me . . . even now I think so.

CLEOSTRATA [*startled*]: She be married to *you*?

LYSIDAMUS: Yes, to me—uh, no, I didn't mean to say that. I wanted to say "to me," but I said "to him."

[*He still doesn't have it right*]

I've got everything completely wrong.

CLEOSTRATA: Indeed you have, and you're not right yet.

LYSIDAMUS: Give her to him

[*Indicates Olympio*]

—No! Wait! To me! Ah, at last I'm back on the right road.

CLEOSTRATA: You run off it too often, my dear.

LYSIDAMUS [*dryly*]: That's what happens when you're trying so hard to get something. But now each of us, this fellow and me,

[*Indicates Olympio*]

recognizing your rights, asks you . . .

CLEOSTRATA: What?

LYSIDAMUS: Well, I'll tell you, my little honey: in reference to this matter of Casina, do this overseer of ours a favor.

CLEOSTRATA: By the gods, I won't do it, nor do I give it my approval.

LYSIDAMUS [*recoiling*]: Then I'll draw out the lots for both sides.

CLEOSTRATA: Who's stopping you?

LYSIDAMUS: I judge rightly that this is the best and fairest thing to do. Afterwards, if things turn out the way we want them to, why, we'll be happy. But if it should turn out some other way, we'll bear up with a calm heart.

[*To Olympio*]

Now take a lot. See what's written on it.

OLYMPIO [*after a long pause for scrutiny*]: One.

CHALINUS: That's not fair! He drew the lots before I did.

LYSIDAMUS [*to Chalinus*]: Now take this one, please.

CHALINUS: Give it to me.

OLYMPIO: Wait a minute! I just now thought of something. See if there is another lot down there in the water.

CHALINUS: You candidate for a whipping post! Do you think I'm like you?

LYSIDAMUS: There, there, that's nothing at all. Keep a level head.

OLYMPIO [*solemnly, in prayer*]: I pray that this turns out well for me, that fortune send. . .

CHALINUS: . . . A BIG DISASTER![10]

OLYMPIO: I do believe that's how it will turn out for you! I know how loyal you are. But wait a minute. Are those lots made out of poplar or fir?

CHALINUS: Why does that worry you?

OLYMPIO: I'm afraid that they might be too light and float to the top.

LYSIDAMUS: Bravo!

[*Then remembers his proper role*]

. . . er, uh, be careful. Throw both lots down together here. There you are. Wife, water!

OLYMPIO: Don't trust your *wife*!

LYSIDAMUS: Cheer up.

OLYMPIO: By the gods, I think she'll jinx the lots if she touches
them!
LYSIDAMUS: Oh, be quiet.
OLYMPIO: I am quiet!

[*Loudly*]

I do call upon the gods. . .
CHALINUS: . . .THAT YOU WEAR AN IRON COLLAR AND BE TIED TO A
WHIPPING POST.
OLYMPIO [*attempting to ignore Chalinus*]:   . . .that it fall out to me by
lot. . .
CHALINUS: . . .THAT YOU HANG UPSIDE-DOWN BY YOUR FEET!
OLYMPIO [*gives up*]:   . . .AND THAT YOUR EYEBALLS BE BLOWN DOWN
YOUR NOSE!

[*Chalinus retreats*]

What are you afraid of? The noose should be ready for you
now.
LYSIDAMUS: Both of you, pay attention to me.
OLYMPIO: I'M QUIET!
LYSIDAMUS: Now, Cleostrata, so that you won't think unkindly of
me or have any suspicions, I'll let you do it. Draw the lots.
OLYMPIO: You're ruining me!
CHALINUS: A bargain.
CLEOSTRATA [*to Lysidamus*]:   Well done.
CHALINUS [*to Olympio*]:   I pray to the gods that your lot fly out of the
urn.
OLYMPIO: Oh, is that so? Because you're a runaway slave, you want
everybody to be like you?
CHALINUS: I hope *your* lot is all mud. I hope it dissolves in the water
just like the clay lots of Hercules' descendants.[11]
OLYMPIO: I hope *you* dissolve. You'll heat up soon enough when the
whip is applied to you.
LYSIDAMUS: Please, Olympio, pay attention.
OLYMPIO: Sure, if this *scholar* here will let me.
LYSIDAMUS [*praying*]:   May this prove to be good and fortunate for
me.
OLYMPIO: Exactly! and good for me too!
CHALINUS [*aside, but loudly*]:   No!
OLYMPIO: No, No! Yes!

CHALINUS: Oh no! Yes for me.

CLEOSTRATA [*points to Chalinus*]: He will win. You'll be sorry.

LYSIDAMUS: Smash that nuisance in the face! Come on, what's wrong?

CLEOSTRATA: Don't you touch him!

OLYMPIO [*calmly, to Lysidamus*]: Should I hit him with my fist or give him a slap?

LYSIDAMUS: Whichever you wish.

OLYMPIO [*strikes Chalinus*]: Take that!

CLEOSTRATA: Why did you hit him?

OLYMPIO: Because my Jupiter ordered me to.

CLEOSTRATA [*to Chalinus*]: Punch him back in the face!

[*Chalinus strikes Olympio*]

OLYMPIO: I'm dead.and buried with blows, Jupiter!

[*To Lysidamus*]

LYSIDAMUS [*to Chalinus*]: What did you hit him for?

CHALINUS: Because my Juno here ordered me to.

LYSIDAMUS [*to Olympio*]: We'll have to put up with this, I'm afraid. My wife seems to have the power.

CLEOSTRATA: My man has just as much right to speak as yours does.

OLYMPIO: Then why did he spoil my prayer with evil omens?

LYSIDAMUS: I advise you to beware of trouble, Chalinus.

CHALINUS [*ruefully*]: Sound advice after all those fists in my face.

LYSIDAMUS: Come now, wife, draw the lots. You two pay attention.

[*Aside*]

I don't know why I'm so afraid! I'm done for! My heart is all aflutter. It's about to leap out. My chest heaves from the labor.

CLEOSTRATA: I've drawn the lot.

LYSIDAMUS: Let's see it!

CHALINUS: Am I done for now?

OLYMPIO: Well, show it. It's in my favor!

CHALINUS: Why don't you drop dead?

[*Grand pause; she throws the lot back in*]

CLEOSTRATA: You *lost*, Chalinus.

LYSIDAMUS: The gods have smiled on us, Olympio. I'm thrilled!

OLYMPIO: Thanks to my Roman piety and my noble ancestors!

LYSIDAMUS: Now go inside, wife. Prepare the marriage ceremony.

CLEOSTRATA: I'll do as you command.

LYSIDAMUS: You realize it's a long way to that farmhouse where he's to take the bride?

[*Points to Olympio*]

CLEOSTRATA: I realize that.

LYSIDAMUS: Then go inside, and even if you don't want to, tend to this promptly.

CLEOSTRATA: Very well.

[*Goes inside*]

LYSIDAMUS [*to Olympio*]:   Let's go inside too, and see that they hurry.

OLYMPIO: Am I stopping you?

[*They go inside*]

LYSIDAMUS [*as he leaves*]:   I certainly don't want to say anything else with this fellow around.

[*Chalinus is left alone on the stage, dejected*]

II.7

CHALINUS [*solo*]:   If I hanged myself now, I'd be wasting the effort. Besides the effort, I'd be going to the expense of a rope and giving my enemies a nice entertainment in the bargain. Why bother anyway? I'm already done for as it is. The lots beat me. Casina will marry the overseer. The worst thing is not that she goes to him but that the old man wanted her so badly to go to the overseer instead of to me. How the wretch trembled! How he scurried about! How he hopped up and down after that overseer stole the show!

[*Hears Lysidamus and Olympio approaching*]

Uh-oh. I'll go over here. I hear the doors opening. My well-wishers and friends are coming outside. From this ambush I'll ambush the both of them.

[*Draws to one side of the stage*]

II.8

[Enter Olympio, dressed in bridegroom's white, with Lysidamus]

OLYMPIO: Just let him come to the country! I'll send him back to you in town tied to a yoke like a charcoal seller.

LYSIDAMUS: That's just the thing to do.

OLYMPIO: I'll see that it's done and taken care of.

LYSIDAMUS: If Chalinus were at home, I'd send him with you to get food so I could pile more misery on top of the pain our enemy already suffers.

CHALINUS *[goes flat against wall]*: I'll draw back against this wall. I'll make like a crab. I've got to catch their conversation on the sly. One of them puts me on the rack, the other twists the screw. Just look at that rascal all dressed in bridegroom's white! That candidate for a whipping! I'll put off dying for now. I aim to send this fellow to Hades ahead of me.

[Freezes into position at one end of the stage; Olympio and Lysidamus are at the other]

OLYMPIO: How pleasant and obedient I've been to you! I've helped you get the thing you most desired. The woman you love will be with you today, and your wife won't know a thing about it.

LYSIDAMUS: Be quiet!

[Looks around]

May the gods love me, I just can't keep my lips off you. I can scarcely keep from kissing you to death. Oh darling![12]

[Tries to embrace Olympio]

CHALINUS *[aside]*: What does he mean "kiss to death"? What's going on? What is this "Oh darling"?

[Lysidamus clutches Olympio]

Ye gods! I think this fellow wants to stretch his overseer's sphincter!

OLYMPIO *[cringing]*: Do you really love me now?

LYSIDAMUS: More than I love myself! Will you let me hug you?

CHALINUS *[aside]*: What? "Hug you"?

OLYMPIO *[shuts eyes; grits teeth]*: All right.

LYSIDAMUS *[embraces him]*: Touching you is as sweet as honey on my tongue!

[Lysidamus clasps Olympio from behind; bumps and grinds]

OLYMPIO: Not on *my* back, loverboy!

[Throws Lysidamus aside]

CHALINUS *[delighted, aside]*:   So that's it! *That's* why he made him his overseer! Once when I escorted him home from a party, he wanted to do the same thing to me—make me his doorman and use *my* door.

[Gestures towards his rear]

OLYMPIO *[trying to get control of situation]*:   What an obliging fellow I've been for you today! What a pleasure!

LYSIDAMUS: Indeed you have. As reward, as long as I live I'll always rate your interests above my own.

CHALINUS *[aside]*:   If you ask me, these two will lock toes before the day is over. This old man seems to prefer grown-up boys.

LYSIDAMUS *[suddenly shifts]*:   Oh, how I'll kiss Casina to death today! Oh the great times I'm going to have without my wife's knowing!

CHALINUS *[aside]*:   Izzatso? Now we're back on the straight and narrow. The same fellow is panting with love for Casina. I'm dealing with men after all!

LYSIDAMUS: Oh, how I long to embrace her and make love!

OLYMPIO *[greatly relieved]*:   But you need to let her get married first.

[Lysidamus struggles towards his house]

Where the devil are you off to now?

LYSIDAMUS *[scarcely able to speak, rasping]*:   I'M IN LOVE.

OLYMPIO: I just don't see how it can happen today.

LYSIDAMUS: It can if you really believe you'll be a free man tomorrow.

CHALINUS *[aside]*:   Now, here's something my ears will have to pay more attention to. I'll cleverly trap two boars in one bush.

LYSIDAMUS: There's a place all ready and waiting at my friend and neighbor's house here.

[Gestures towards Alcesimus's house]

I've entrusted him with the whole story of my love. He said he'd give me a room for it.

OLYMPIO: What about his wife? Where will she be?

LYSIDAMUS: I've fixed that quite nicely. My wife will call her over
here for the wedding so she can keep her company and spend
the night. I ordered this to be done, and my wife said she
would do it. Myrrhina will sleep here. I'll see to it that her
husband stays out of the house. You'll bring the bride to the
country, all right, but the *country* will be *here*.

[*Obscene gestures towards his crotch*]

at least as long as it takes for me to consummate my marriage
with Casina. Then tomorrow morning you'll take her to the
country. Isn't that clever?

OLYMPIO: Well planned.

CHALINUS [*aside*]:   Go on, then, hatch your plots. You'll be sorry you
wore out your wits on all this.

LYSIDAMUS: Now, do you know what you're supposed to do?

[*Olympio nods and runs off; realizing that he does not know, then, he returns*]

OLYMPIO: Tell me.

LYSIDAMUS: Take this purse. Go off and buy food. Hurry, now! But
I want it nice. The softest little tidbits, since she herself is the
softest little titbit.

OLYMPIO: All right.

LYSIDAMUS [*licking his chops*]:   Buy fish: cuttlefish, squid, limpets,
well-bred fish . . .

CHALINUS [*interrupting, aside*]:   No, breaded fish if you're smart.

LYSIDAMUS: . . . and sole.

CHALINUS [*again interrupting, aside*]:   Why buy only the sole when
you could buy the whole sandal? With that we could tenderize
your whole face, you dirty old man.

OLYMPIO: Do you want any tongue fish?

[*Wiggles tongue obscenely*]

LYSIDAMUS: What do I need with that when I've got a wife at home
already? She's my tongue fish. She never shuts up.

OLYMPIO: When I get there, I can ask the fishmonger what I should
buy.

LYSIDAMUS: That's a good idea. Now, be off! Money's no object.
Buy plenty of food. Now I have to see my neighbor to make
sure he'll do what I've asked him to.

OLYMPIO: May I go now?

LYSIDAMUS: Yes.

[*Exit Olympio; Lysidamus enters the houe of Alcesimus*]

CHALINUS [*solo*]:   If I were freed three times over, it wouldn't keep
    me from plotting some horrible evil for those two today! I'm
    going to reveal everything to my mistress—the whole plot. I
    have my enemies in a trap. If she will do her duty, the whole
    contest will be ours. I'll pass those fellows at a pretty pace. The
    day is running our way: we the conquered have conquered.
    Now, inside to season what one cook has already seasoned
    one way, another way.

[*Pauses*]

    What was once prepared will now be unprepared,
    and what was not prepared before will now be prepared.

[*Scampers into the house of Lysidamus*]

III.1

[*Enter Lysidamus with Alcesimus from Alcesimus's house*]

LYSIDAMUS: Now, Alcesimus, we'll see whether you're a true friend
    or enemy.
    Now the end in sight is sighted,
    now the decision is decided.
    As for finding fault with why I'm in love,
    stash that away in your purse and save it.
    "Gray hair," you say? "Different ages"? Stash that away.
    "A man with a wife"? Stash that away too.

ALCESIMUS [*cackling*]:   I've never seen a man more wretched from
    love than you.

LYSIDAMUS: See that your house is empty.

ALCESIMUS: Even the household slaves are gone. I ordered the
    maids to go over to your place.

LYSIDAMUS: Oh, how knowingly knowledgeable you are! But see
    that they do what any birds do who have to make a long
    migration: let them go cawing with their crops filled with
    goodies for a far-flung flight to the frontier.[13]

ALCESIMUS: I'll keep that in mind.

LYSIDAMUS: That's settled! You're really a clever fellow. You don't need a public decree to show your pedigree. Take care of everything here. I'm going off to the forum now. Then right back home.

ALCESIMUS: Have a nice trip.

LYSIDAMUS [*comes back*]:   By the way, see to it that your house has its tongue in its cheek.

ALCESIMUS: What do you mean?

LYSIDAMUS: When I return, I won't have time for anything that needs depressing.

[*Cackles*]

ALCESIMUS: Whooee! You're going to be cut down to size. You make too many puns.

LYSIDAMUS: What good would it be for me to be in love if I weren't smart and quick of wit?

[*Leaps up and down in delight*]

But see to it, now, that I don't have to go looking for you.

ALCESIMUS: I'll be here at home.

[*Lysidamus departs; Alcesimus goes into his house*]

III.2

[*Cleostrata enters*]

CLEOSTRATA: So...SO! By the gods, *this* is what my lord and master begged for so eagerly! To hurry out to call my neighbor *there* over to my house here.

[*Points*]

That way their house could be empty and he could take Casina there. That's just why I'm *not* going to call her. What? Give those old wretches a chance at a free playroom? Those randy, rutting old rams!

[*Enter Alcesimus*]

But look! Here comes that pillar of the senate, the people's protector, my neighbor, the fellow who offered a free house to my husband. He's not worth a pinch of salt.

ALCESIMUS: I wonder why my wife hasn't been invited next-door yet. She's been dressed up and sitting at home for some time, just waiting to be invited. But look! Here's her invitation. Greetings, Cleostrata.

CLEOSTRATA: And greetings to you, Alcesimus. Where is your wife?

ALCESIMUS: She's waiting to see whether or not you'll invite her. Your husband asked me to send her to you to help you out. You want me to call her?

CLEOSTRATA: No, don't bother her if she's busy.

ALCESIMUS: Oh, she's free now . . .

CLEOSTRATA: Oh, I don't really care. I don't want to be a bother to her. I'll meet her later.

ALCESIMUS: Haven't you been getting ready for the marriage?

CLEOSTRATA: Yes, so much decoration and preparation.

ALCESIMUS: Don't you need a helping hand or two?

CLEOSTRATA: There's enough help at home. When it's time for the wedding I'll see her.

[*In sweetest possible tones*]

Now, farewell, and give my *very* best greetings to your wife.

[*Goes towards her house, but pauses to watch Alcesimus*]

ALCESIMUS [*aside, in desperation*]:   Now what will I do? I've made a complete mess of everything! And all because of the business that dirty, toothless old goat got me into. I promised my wife's help, practically got her to wash dishes, for that disgrace of a man, who tells me his wife is going to invite her

[*Gestures towards his house*]

over there. And she

[*Points to Lysidamus's house*]

claims that she doesn't have a care in the world. I'd be surprised if this doesn't mean my neighbor's wife has sniffed him out. No, when I reckon up the accounts, if anything like that had happened, there would already be a claim against me. I'll go inside, then, and put my own ship into dry dock.

[*Goes into his house*]

CLEOSTRATA [*comes forward*]:   Now there's a fellow who's been finely fooled. How these wretches do rush around! Now that I've finished that one off, I wish that worthless, decrepit husband of mine would come out and take his turn at being made a fool. What I intend to do is start some kind of quarrel between those two.

[*Enter Lysidamus*]

Well, now look! Here he comes. With a look that solemn, you'd think he was an honest man.

III.3

[*Enter Lysidamus from forum, not seeing Cleostrata*]

LYSIDAMUS: What a stupid thing to do, and *my* idea too! For any man in love to run off to the forum on business on the very day that he has something available to make love to! That's just what I did, fool that I am. I've wasted the day while I stood by as an advocate for a relative of mine. I'm delighted that he lost his case so that he didn't need my services for a trial today—too bad if he had anyway. Anyone who calls a counselor to counsel should first find out whether the counselor has his heart in it, body and soul—otherwise let him go home, solo.

[*Sees Cleostrata*]

But there's my wife in front of our house! Heaven help me! I'm afraid she's not deaf and has heard everything.
CLEOSTRATA [*aside*]:   By the gods, I heard what you said, all right, you with your evil plotting.
LYSIDAMUS: I'll go nearer. How are you, my delight?
CLEOSTRATA [*sweetly*]:   Why, dear, I've been waiting for you.
LYSIDAMUS: Is everything all arranged now? Are you going to bring over our neighbor's wife to help you?
CLEOSTRATA: I invited her, as you commanded me. But that comrade of yours, your excellent friend, has gotten a little annoyed with his wife. He says he won't send her if *I* invite her.
LYSIDAMUS: That's your worst fault: you're not very seductive, you know.
CLEOSTRATA: It's not a wife's duty, my dear husband, to entice other women's husbands. That's a job for whores. *You* go and invite her!

[*Lysidamus is startled*]

> I want to look after what needs to be done inside our house, my darling husband.

LYSIDAMUS: Well, hurry up, then.

CLEOSTRATA: As you wish.

[*Aside, acidly*]

> Now, by god, I'll throw a little fear into his heart. I'll have one miserable loverboy on my hands before this day's over!

[*Goes inside*]

III.4
[*Enter Alcesimus from his house*]

ALCESIMUS [*to himself*]: I've come back to see whether our lover has come home yet from the forum. You know, the fellow who made a fool of me and my wife—the madman? But there he is in front of his house. By Hercules, I'll go right up to you.

LYSIDAMUS: And, by Hercules, I'm doing the same to you. What do you have to say for yourself, you worthless bum? What did I order you to do? What did I *plead* with you to do?

ALCESIMUS: What do you mean?

LYSIDAMUS: What a nice job you did emptying out your house for me! How carefully you brought your wife over to our house! Thanks to you, I'm ruined, and so are my chances.

ALCESIMUS: What do you mean? Why don't you go hang yourself? You just told me that your wife would invite my wife to come over.

LYSIDAMUS: But she said she had invited her, and she said *you* said you weren't going to send her.

ALCESIMUS: Well now,[14] she told me herself she didn't mind doing what was assigned her—that's her job.

LYSIDAMUS

> Well, she ordered me to call her now.

ALCESIMUS

> Well, as if I cared now.

LYSIDAMUS

> Well now, you're ruining me.

ALCESIMUS

> Well now, that's just fine.

Well now, I want you to. . . WELL NOW!
do something pleasant, and do it willingly.
You won't have any more "well nows"
today than I will.
Well now! for the very last time,
may the gods destroy you!

LYSIDAMUS
Well, NOW WHAT?
Will you send your wife over to my wife?

ALCESIMUS
You can marry her if you want to!
You can go to hell and back
a hundred times if you want to!
With her, your wife, your girl friend!

Go on, now, and tend to your other business. I'll order my
wife to cross over through our garden to visit your wife.

LYSIDAMUS: Now you're the kind of friend a man should really
have.

[*Alcesimus goes into his house*]

What brought this love to my heart? Was it a Roman omen?
What was it I did to offend Venus? Why does she make so
many delays for me and my love?

[*Uproar, tragic, inside Lysidamus's house*]

What's that? Oh, oh. What is that uproar inside our house?

III.5

[*Pardalisca comes onstage accompanied by groaning servants acting as a
chorus: she declaims in the manner of tragic heroine*][15]

PARDALISCA
Undone I am! Alas I am undone!
All of me in ruins! All, I say!
Heart through fear stops beating,
poor wretched limbs all atremble.
Whence the aid of refuge, rescue, restoration?
I know no source at hand.
Such strange things have I seen within
accomplished all in wondrous wise!

Oh new and unheard-of audacity!
Be thou ware, Cleostrata! Oh take ye care!
Take thyself from out her sight, I pray,
lest she, rampant in her rage,
bring some evil in thy way.
OH, SNATCH FROM HER THE SWORD
THAT IS SO SORELY VEXED IN WITS!

LYSIDAMUS [*stunned*]:   Why, what can be the reason for her leaping
out here so scared and out of breath? Pardalisca!

PARDALISCA
I am undone . . .

[*In a daze, looks about as if waking from nightmare*]

But whence do mine ears acquire
the tone of another's voice?

LYSIDAMUS: Look over this way.

PARDALISCA
Oh, master mine . . .

LYSIDAMUS: What's the matter? Why are you so frightened?

PARDALISCA
I am undone!

LYSIDAMUS
What do you mean, *you are undone?*

PARDALISCA [*as if conjugating a verb*]
I am undone . . . YOU are undone . . .

LYSIDAMUS
Oh, no! *I too am undone!*

[*Catches the tragic strain*]

Well, alas how so?

PARDALISCA
Woe be unto you!

LYSIDAMUS: On the contrary, I would prefer woe apply to you.

PARDALISCA
Hold me, please, lest I fall!

LYSIDAMUS: Whatever is the matter? Tell me quickly!

PARDALISCA
Hold up my bosom! Fan me, please, with your cloak!

LYSIDAMUS [*aside*]:   I'm afraid to find out what all this business may
be about . . . unless she's pickled herself with the blossoms of
Bacchus.

PARDALISCA: Please hold my ears.

[*Suggestively puckers her lips*]

LYSIDAMUS [*drops her to the floor*]: You can go from me straight to the cross! May the gods ruin your bosom, your ears, your head, and you! If I don't find out at once what this is all about, I'll scatter your brains all over the floor with this!

[*Threatens with his cane*]

You viper! You've done nothing but make a fool of me so far!

PARDALISCA [*persists in tragic style*]
Oh, master mine...

LYSIDAMUS [*mimics her angrily*]
What is it, *oh maidservant mine?*

PARDALISCA: You're too mean to me.

LYSIDAMUS: You're exactly right there. But tell me what this is all about, and do it in a few words. What is all that noise inside?

PARDALISCA: You shall know. Listen.

[*In matter-of-fact style*]

Your maid began to raise trouble inside our house. Yes, a great deal of trouble, and this is what she did

[*As an afterthought*]

—not at all befitting one of decent Greek upbringing.

LYSIDAMUS: Well, what did she do?

PARDALISCA [*slips back into tragic style; servants moan*]
FEAR FETTERS THE TALE OF MY TONGUE!

[*Clutches her throat*]

LYSIDAMUS: Can I *ever* learn from you what is going on?

PARDALISCA: I shall tell you.

[*Again in normal voice*]

Your servant, whom you want to give as a wife to your overseer.

[*Lapses back into tragic style*]

She...within...

LYSIDAMUS: *What* within? What is it?

PARDALISCA

She follows the evil example of wicked women.
She threatens her husband, his life . . .

[*Trails off, as if the prophetic vision is fading*]

LYSIDAMUS: Well, what does she threaten?

PARDALISCA

Alas . . .

LYSIDAMUS: What is it?

PARDALISCA

She says she wants to deprive him of his life!
A sword . . .

[*Again the "vision" fades*]

LYSIDAMUS: What?

PARDALISCA [*squints into the distance*]

A sword . . .

LYSIDAMUS: What about a sword?

PARDALISCA [*in a flat voice, disgusted at his obtuseness*]:   She has one.

LYSIDAMUS: Heaven help me! Why does she have it?

PARDALISCA

She's running through every room of the house.
She will let no one come near her.
That's why everyone is hiding under the chests,
under the beds. SPEECHLESS WITH TERROR THEY TREMBLE.

[*The chorus of servants moans again*]

LYSIDAMUS: I'm dead and done for. What evil thing was it that
came upon her so suddenly?

PARDALISCA [*with eyes open wide*]

She's . . . gone . . . MAD . . .

LYSIDAMUS: I believe I'm the unluckiest man who ever lived.

PARDALISCA

Oh, if you only knew what words she said today!

LYSIDAMUS: I would like to know them—today. What did she say?

PARDALISCA: Listen.

[*Back into tragic style*]

> By all the gods and goddesses she swore
> she'd slay him who this night did with her lie.[16]

LYSIDAMUS: She'd kill *me*?[17]

PARDALISCA [*drops into normal voice, puzzled*]: Why, goodness me! Does this have anything to do with you?

LYSIDAMUS: Oops!

PARDALISCA: What is your concern with her?

LYSIDAMUS: I made a mistake. I wanted to say something else. My overseer . . .

PARDALISCA [*aside to audience*]: He knows full well he's off the road and on a detour!

LYSIDAMUS: She didn't really threaten me?

PARDALISCA [*in normal voice*]: She's more angry at you than at anyone else.

LYSIDAMUS: Why?

PARDALISCA [*briskly*]: Because you're marrying her to Olympio, she won't allow your life or her own life *or* that of her husband to be prolonged another day. I've been sent here to tell you.

[*Again, Cassandra-like*]

> . . . be on your guard!

LYSIDAMUS: Oh gods, I'm ruined! Poor me.

PARDALISCA [*aside, to audience*]: You deserve to be.

LYSIDAMUS: There is not now, nor has there ever been, an old man in love more wretched than me.

PARDALISCA [*aside, to audience*]: I'm stringing him along so cleverly! Everything I've told him was nothing but a lie. My mistress and her friend from next-door invented this trick. I was sent to play it on him.

[*Resumes tragic pose*]

LYSIDAMUS: Now, see here, Pardalisca.

PARDALISCA: Yes, what is it?

LYSIDAMUS: There's something . . .

PARDALISCA: What?

LYSIDAMUS: There's something I want to ask you about.

PARDALISCA: You're delaying me.

LYSIDAMUS: And you're slaying me. But tell me, does Casina have the sword even now?

PARDALISCA: She does.

[*Brightly*]

> In fact, she has *two*.

LYSIDAMUS: What! Two?

PARDALISCA: She says she'll kill you with one of them today, and then kill your overseer with the other.

LYSIDAMUS: I'm the deadest of all men alive. I think I'd better put on a breastplate. But what of my wife? Didn't she go up and take the swords away?

PARDALISCA: No one dares come near her.

LYSIDAMUS: Let her beg for them, then.

PARDALISCA: She is begging. But Casina refuses to cooperate in any way unless she knows that she won't be given to the overseer.

LYSIDAMUS: Well, she'll get married today even if she doesn't want to, for the simple reason that she doesn't want to. Why don't I finish what I started to do? She could marry *me*—I mean I wanted to say, our overseer.

PARDALISCA: You make that little error often enough, don't you?

LYSIDAMUS [*sarcastically*]: "FEAR FETTERS THE TALE OF MY TONGUE." But please get my wife to plead with her to put aside the sword and let me come back into the house.

PARDALISCA: I'll take the message.

LYSIDAMUS: Be sure you ask her.

PARDALISCA: I'll be sure to ask her.

LYSIDAMUS: And be sure to ask her winningly, as is your custom. But listen now:

[*In rapid, cheerful style, as Pardalisca scampers into house*]

> *Get this done and on your foot*
> *a freedman's sandal shall be put,*
> *a ring of gold upon your hand*
> *and lots of gold at your command.*

PARDALISCA

> *I'll see to it.*

LYSIDAMUS

> *See that you do.*
> *Get what I want.*

PARDALISCA

> *I'll tell her true*
> *if I am not*
> *detained by you!*

LYSIDAMUS
> *Be off, be off!*
> *See that you do. Shoo!*

[*Exit Pardalisca*]

LYSIDAMUS [*sees Olympio returning*]:   But look! My helper is returning with the goods. He's leading a parade.

III.6

[*Enter Olympio and Citrio with a train of cooks, attendants, and food*]

OLYMPIO: See to it that you keep your thorns in line, you thief.
CITRIO: Why are these fellows thorns?
OLYMPIO: Whatever they touch they snare at once. If you go to take it back, they break right off. The same thing happens when they go anywhere. They do their masters double damage.
CITRIO: Oh, go on...
OLYMPIO: Wait a minute!

[*Sees Lysidamus*]

> Now I'll dress myself up in grand, aristocratic style and go greet my master.

LYSIDAMUS: Good day, my fine fellow.
OLYMPIO: I must admit I am.
LYSIDAMUS: How are things going?
OLYMPIO: You're in love; I'm hungry and thirsty.
LYSIDAMUS: You've made quite an elegant entrance.
OLYMPIO: Ah, I don't need you today...make love on your own.
LYSIDAMUS [*draws near him*]:   Wait a minute, you with all your airs.
OLYMPIO: Pee-yew! Your conversation stinks.
LYSIDAMUS: What's the matter?
OLYMPIO: This is the matter.

[*Points to provisions*]

LYSIDAMUS: Won't you come closer?
OLYMPIO [*like a street tough*]:   Come on, man. Don't gimme a hard time![18]
LYSIDAMUS [*advances again*]:   You're gonna get it, see, if you don't come here.
OLYMPIO: OH ZEUS! OZONE! Would you please keep away from me? Do you want me to throw up right now?

[*Moves away*]

LYSIDAMUS: Wait...

OLYMPIO: What is it?

[*With mock wonder to the bystanders*]

Who is this man?

[*Points to Lysidamus*]

LYSIDAMUS: Why, I'm your master!

OLYMPIO: Whose master?

LYSIDAMUS: The one whose slave you are.

OLYMPIO: *Me* a slave?

LYSIDAMUS: Yes, *my* slave.

OLYMPIO: I'm not free? Think again, think again!

LYSIDAMUS [*tries to embrace him*]: Wait, stand still!

OLYMPIO: Stop that!

LYSIDAMUS [*suddenly remembers what he's really after*]: I am your slave.

OLYMPIO: That's much better.

LYSIDAMUS: I beg you, Olympio-lady, my father, my paterfamilias, my patron...

OLYMPIO: Ah...you *do* have taste!

LYSIDAMUS [*falls to his knees*]: I really am yours.

OLYMPIO: What do I need with such a worthless slave?

LYSIDAMUS: What now?

[*Swoons*]

How soon will you feed my desire?

OLYMPIO: I wish the dinner were finished cooking now.

LYSIDAMUS: Have these fellows go off and tend to it, then.

OLYMPIO [*to cooks*]: Quick, go inside and get the dinner ready. I'll go inside now myself. See to it that my meal is soused in sauce. Oh, but I want to dine elegantly and neatly. None of that Roman-style fodder for me.[19]

[*They go inside; to Lysidamus*]

Are you still here? Why don't you go in?

LYSIDAMUS: You go. I'm staying here.

OLYMPIO: Is there anything else that might be keeping you back?

LYSIDAMUS: She...

[*Points to Pardalisca's exit door*]

    says that Casina is inside the house with a sword. She says
    she's going to kill you and me.

OLYMPIO: Oh, sure...that's fine for her. They're fiddling over
    trifles. I know what those demons are like, all right. Why not
    go inside with me?

LYSIDAMUS: By the gods, I'm afraid something's wrong. You go
    inside, though. Find out what's going on.

OLYMPIO: My life is just as dear to me as yours is to you. Come
    along, now.

LYSIDAMUS [*reluctantly*]: If you say so. Here's company for you.

[*They enter the house*]

IV.1

[*Enter Pardalisca, laughing*]

PARDALISCA: By the gods, I don't believe they have as festive games
    at Nemea or Olympia as the gamey games we're playing
    inside on our household's old man and our overseer Olym-
    pio. Everybody's running around inside the house; the old
    man's shouting in the kitchen, urging on the cooks: "Why
    don't you get on with it? Why don't you produce the food if
    you're going to produce it? Hurry up! Dinner should have
    been cooked by now!" And the overseer is walking around
    with a wreath on his brow, all in white, scrubbed and dressed
    fit to kill. Those two women are dressing Chalinus, to give
    him in marriage to our overseer in place of Casina. But
    they've covered all this up very cleverly, as if they didn't know
    anything about what is going to happen. The cooks have seen
    to it that the old man won't eat. It's too clever for words!
    They're turning over the pots and throwing water on the fire.
    They're doing all of this at the request of the women. What
    they want to do is drive the old man out of the house without
    his dinner; once they're alone they can stuff their bellies. I
    know those greedy women. They can devour whole shiploads
    of food. But the door is opening.

IV.2

[*Enter Lysidamus from his house*]

LYSIDAMUS [to Cleostrata, within]:   If you take my advice, wife, you women will go ahead and dine as soon as dinner is ready. I'll have my dinner in the country. I want to follow the new bridegroom and his new bride out there. I know only too well what wicked men can do. I don't want anyone running off with her. Have a good time. Now hurry and send the two of them out at once. We must get there while it's still light. I'll be back tomorrow. Tomorrow, wife, I'll have myself a banquet.

PARDALISCA [aside]:   Just what I said would happen is happening. The women are kicking the old man outside without his supper.

LYSIDAMUS [to Pardalisca]:   What are you doing here?

PARDALISCA: I'm going where my mistress sent me.

LYSIDAMUS: Oh, is that so?

PARDALISCA: I'm late.

LYSIDAMUS: What are you looking for here?

PARDALISCA: I'm not looking for anything.

LYSIDAMUS: Off with you! Here you are lingering around outside while everybody else is rushing around inside.

PARDALISCA: I'm off.

[Goes to house]

LYSIDAMUS: Then be off, you horrible whore!

[She goes into the house]

Has she gone at last? Now I can say what I please. A man in love needs no food, not even if he's hungry. But look who's coming now with nuptial wreath and bridal torch! My ally, my equal, my fellow hubby bridegroom, my overseer!

IV.3

[Enter Olympio with flute player]

OLYMPIO: This way, flute player. When they bring this new bride out of doors, fill the entire street with the sweet sound of my wedding song.

[Sings]

Oh, wedding hymn,
dear wedding hymn . . .

LYSIDAMUS: What now, my savior?

OLYMPIO: I'm starving, by the gods, and I don't think I'm saving myself at all.

LYSIDAMUS: But I'm in love!

OLYMPIO: But I don't care, damn it. Love is food enough for you. As for me, my guts are already rumbling from starvation.

LYSIDAMUS: Now, why are those slowpokes delaying inside so? It's as though the more I rush around, the less gets done.

OLYMPIO: Then what if I sing the wedding song? Maybe that would make things go faster.

LYSIDAMUS: That's fine. Do it. I'll help you. We'll have a joint ceremony.

[*Flute gives clue*]

LYSIDAMUS AND OLYMPIO [*together, harmonizing*]:
   Oh wedding hymn, dear wedding hymn . . .

[*Olympio keeps his note going during following speech*]

LYSIDAMUS: Gods, I'm ruined, wretch that I am. What does it matter if I bust a gut singing the wedding song? There's no chance I'll get to bust the gut I want to.

OLYMPIO [*stops singing*]:   Indeed. If you were a horse, you'd be untamable.

LYSIDAMUS: How do you figure that?

OLYMPIO: You're too unbridled.

[*Lysidamus winces*]

LYSIDAMUS [*advances*]:   Have you ever felt me to be too unbridled?

OLYMPIO [*backs off*]:   Gods forbid! Wait! The door's opening. They're coming outside.

LYSIDAMUS: Ah, the gods want to save me after all!

PARDALISCA [*enters; to audience, noting Lysidamus's excitement*]:   He has a whiff from afar of this male Casina.

IV.4

[*A bridal procession enters; Chalinus minces in, with veil over face; he is dressed as a bride, accompanied by servants, Cleostrata, and Myrrhina*]

PARDALISCA [*singing*]
   High over door's
   threshold lift high,

come, my young bride,
lift your feet oh so high.

Long may you live,
journey's begun,
so may you outlive
your man number one.

Waxing in power,
winning in might,
weaving your webs of
widow's delight.

You'll beat your husband
every time you fight him.
Outtalk him,
outshout him:
that's now your custom.

He'll dress you well.
Take all he owns.
Both days and nights
plot his next overthrow.

[*The rest of the entourage join in*]

Be sly, I pray,
in every way.
Keep this commandment,
I . . .

[*Olympio breaks in*]

OLYMPIO: She'll be up to her neck in trouble, and at once, if she makes the least little mistake!
LYSIDAMUS: Hush!

[*Indicates procession*]

OLYMPIO: I won't shut up.
LYSIDAMUS: What's the matter?
OLYMPIO: One wicked woman is waking wickedness in another.
LYSIDAMUS: You're going to undo everything that's been done.

That's what they hope and pray for: to undo all that we've done so far.

CLEOSTRATA: Come now, Olympio,

[*Suppresses laughter*]

take this wife from us whenever you wish.

OLYMPIO: Then give her to me, if you're going to do it today.

LYSIDAMUS [*to maids*]: You two go inside.

CLEOSTRATA [*suppressing laughter*]: And please treat this innocent, untouched maiden gently.

OLYMPIO: Certainly. Fare you well.

LYSIDAMUS: Go inside, you two, go inside.

CLEOSTRATA: Good day to you then.

[*The members of the procession go inside in gales of laughter*]

LYSIDAMUS: Is my wife inside yet?

OLYMPIO: She's in the house, don't worry.

LYSIDAMUS: Hooray! Whoopee! Now at long last I'm a free man. My little heart.

[*Draws near "Casina"*]

My little honey-woney...my little springy-wingy...

[*"Casina" giggles demurely in falsetto*]

OLYMPIO: Listen, if you have any sense, you'll keep clear of trouble. This girl is mine.

[*Tries to drag "Casina" off; she squeals*]

LYSIDAMUS: I know, but I get to have her first.

[*Drags her the other way; more squeals*]

OLYMPIO: You hold the wedding torch.

LYSIDAMUS: No, I'd rather hold *her* instead.

[*Holds "Casina"; more girlish squeals; Lysidamus prays to heaven*]

Oh Venus omnipotent, how many blessings you gave me when you gave me possession of her.

OLYMPIO: Oh, your tender little iddy-biddy bodikins!

[*"Casina" giggles again*]

my wittle wifey-poo.

[*"Casina" stomps on his foot*]

OUCH! What on earth!

LYSIDAMUS: What's the matter?

OLYMPIO [*hopping around*]: She stomped on my foot like an elephant!

LYSIDAMUS: Oh, keep quiet. No cloud is as downy as her breast.

OLYMPIO [*caresses "Casina"s' breasts*]: Oh, what pretty little knobby-wobbies—

[*"Casina" elbows him in the stomach*]

Ouch! Oh misery!

LYSIDAMUS: What's wrong?

OLYMPIO: She struck me in the chest! She's got an elbow like a battering ram!

LYSIDAMUS: Now, Olympio, I ask you, why are you being so rough with her? When *I* touch this little belle, she's never bellicose.

[*"Casina" elbows him in the stomach*]

Ouch!

OLYMPIO: What's the matter with *you?*

LYSIDAMUS: My goodness, what a strong little thing she is! She almost laid me out with that elbow.

OLYMPIO: That means she wants to get laid out herself.

[*More giggles from "Casina" at this wit*]

LYSIDAMUS: What are we waiting for? Let's go in!

OLYMPIO: Come along sweetly, sweety.

[*All three enter the house of Alcesimus; one last squeal from "Casina"*]

V.1

[*Enter Myrrhina, Pardalisca, and Cleostrata from the house of Lysidamus*]

MYRRHINA: We've had a good time inside, and now we've come outside to see the wedding games. By the gods, never have I laughed as much as this. I don't think I'll ever laugh this much again as long as I live!

PARDALISCA: Wouldn't it be nice to know what Chalinus is doing? to know what the new bride is doing with *his* husband?

MYRRHINA: No playwright ever put together a plot craftier than the fabulous fable we've created.

CLEOSTRATA: I want to see the old man now with his face smashed in, to tell him no one more wicked ever lived—unless you think the man who offered him a room for his debauchery is wicked too. I want you to take over now, Pardalisca. Make a fool of any man who comes outside.

PARDALISCA: I'll do that gladly, just as I usually do.

CLEOSTRATA: Watch everything they do inside. Take your place behind me, now.

MYRRHINA: That way you can say what you want to as boldly as you please.

CLEOSTRATA: Quiet now, someone is coming out.

[*They hide in Cleostrata's doorway*]

V.2

[*Enter Olympio from house of Alcesimus, disheveled*][20]

OLYMPIO: Where can I run to? Where can I hide? How can I escape the disgrace? I don't know. My master and I have outdone ourselves with this marriage. I'm ashamed. I'm afraid. We're both of us laughing stocks. What a fool I am! Say, that's something new for me! A fellow embarrassed who has never embarrassed before.

[*Addresses audience*]

Now, pay attention while I tell you what happened to me. Listen closely. It's worth your trouble.

[*Throughout the speech Olympio mimes the events he describes*]

It's so ridiculous for you to hear, and me to repeat, what a disturbance I caused in there. After I'd led this new bride inside, I took her straight to the bedroom. It was as dark in there as the bottom of a well. Since the old man wasn't there yet, I said "Lie down." I got her in position, I propped her on a pillow, I softened her up, I said flattering things to her. That way I could have my wedding before the old man had his. I started off a little slow at first because I kept expecting the old man to surprise us. I asked her to kiss me, to get the ball rolling, so to speak. She knocked my hand away and wouldn't even let me kiss her. But I pressed home eagerly. More than ever I was ready to enter Casina. I wanted to relieve the old man of that task. I shut the door so he wouldn't catch me by surprise.

CLEOSTRATA [*to Pardalisca*]:   Come on, now, go over to him.

PARDALISCA [*goes over to Olympio*]:   Tell me, where is that new bride of yours?

OLYMPIO [*startled to see witnesses onstage*]:   Oh Hercules, I'm done for! The plot's discovered.

PARDALISCA: Then it's only fair you confess the whole thing, and in proper order. What happened inside? What did Casina do? Was she obedient enough for you?

OLYMPIO: It's *so* embarrassing!

PARDALISCA: Tell the whole thing in order, the way you started to.

OLYMPIO: Oh, it's *so* embarrassing!

PARDALISCA: Come, now, be bold! After you got in bed—I want you to tell me what happened.

OLYMPIO: It's *so* disgraceful!

PARDALISCA: Everybody who hears you will see to it that they are not corrupted by your tale.

OLYMPIO: It was so big. . .

PARDALISCA: You're stalling. Won't you go on?

OLYMPIO: I reached all the way under her dress, and I found. . .

PARDALISCA: What?

OLYMPIO: Oo-la-la!

PARDALISCA: What?

OLYMPIO: Um, um, um!

[*Shakes his head*]

PARDALISCA: What did you find?

OLYMPIO: Oh, the most *enormous* thing! I was afraid she might have a sword. I began to search for it. One thing I didn't need in bed under me was a sword. While I was searching to make sure she didn't have one, I put my hands on a. . . a. . . handle. But now that I think about it, she didn't have a sword: *that* would have been cold.

PARDALISCA: Do go on.

OLYMPIO: But it's *so* embarrassing!

PARDALISCA: It wasn't a *horse-radish*, was it?

OLYMPIO: No.

PARDALISCA: It wasn't a *cucumber*, was it?

OLYMPIO: By the gods, there's no telling what it was, except that it wasn't any kind of vegetable. One thing is clear: whatever it was, no blight had touched it. Yes indeed. Whatever it was, it was fully grown.

PARDALISCA: What happened then? Tell me.

OLYMPIO: I called softly to Casina. I said, "Please, little wifey mine, why are you rejecting me, your husband? It's really unfair, doing this to me. I'm the one who won you, you know." She didn't say a word. She covered the place where you are women with her dress. When I saw that pasture fenced off, I asked her to let me try another field. I asked her to be nice and roll over. She didn't let out a peep. She just lay there, never saying a thing. I tried to kiss her, tried to lift her lovely legs up in the air . . .

MYRRHINA [*aside, to audience*]:   He's telling it all so charmingly, just as charmingly as can be, and the joke's on him!

OLYMPIO: I thought I might at least get a kiss from her. But the beard on her lips scratched my cheeks like a bristle. I got up on my knees at once, and she struck me in the chest with her feet! I fell headlong off the bed. She punched me in the face. That's when I ran out of there, without making so much as a sound, and wearing the very clothes I've got on. Now the old man can have a drink from the same cup I drank from.

PARDALISCA: That's perfect. But where is your little cloak?

OLYMPIO: I left it inside there.

PARDALISCA: Well, now, do you think you've had enough clever tricks played on you for one day?

OLYMPIO: And how! Oh no! the door's opening! I hope she's not following me!

V.3

[*Enter Lysidamus from Alcesimus's house without his cloak*]

LYSIDAMUS [*noticing no one else, runs around in circles*]
   My shame sets me on fire
   with my thwarted desire!
   What more can I do
   with my life all askew?
   The very sight of my wife
   would send me straight to the knife.

Why, I don't even dare look in her face!
I'm dead and done for, a total disgrace.
She's got me by the throat, plainly!
I'll struggle hard, but oh how vainly!

[*Turns to audience*]

I wish I knew how to clear myself with her. And here I am, poor me, without a cloak, all because of the wedding I tried to have on the sly. Well, I suppose there's nothing else to do but confess. That's probably the best course now. I'll go inside and offer my back to my wife for a beating.

[*Starts to go inside, then turns back to audience*]

Or is there someone of you here who would like to do that job for me?

[*Resumes*]

I don't know what to do now, except to be like a wicked slave and run away from home. There's no salvation for these shoulders if I stay here.

[*Changes his mind again; turns back to house*]

Oh, that's all a lot of nonsense. Pay it no mind. By the gods, I'll get flogged. But if I deserve it, that doesn't mean I like it. I'll go off this way at once!

[*Starts to run away again, Chalinus comes running out of house, still dressed as a bride*]

CHALINUS: Stop right there, loverboy!
LYSIDAMUS: I'm doomed! I'm called back! I'll slip off now and pretend I didn't hear.

[*Starts to tiptoe away*]

V.4

CHALINUS: Where do you think you're going? You want to imitate the degenerate ways of the Greeks, eh? Want to get under me again? Here's your chance. Go back into the bedroom if you want to. You're finished. Step this way now. I'll find a fair arbitrator for you—outside the courtroom.

[*Gestures with club*]

LYSIDAMUS: This is the end! That fellow will shave my shanks with that cudgel of his.

[*Turns in other direction*]

I'll have to escape this way. *That* way is blocked off by that bat-bearing ball buster.

[*Runs into Cleostrata*]

CLEOSTRATA: A very good day to you, loverboy.

LYSIDAMUS [*shrieks*]: Oh, no! My wife blocks the way! Now I'm between the altar and the sacrificial blade, and I don't know where I can flee. *Wolves* on one side,

[*Gestures towards Chalinus*]

dogs on the other.

[*Gestures towards Cleostrata*]

But the wolf is armed with a club. I think I'll have to reserve the old proverb and go this way. I hope a bitch's bark won't be as bad as a wolf's bite!

CLEOSTRATA [*blocks his way*]: What are you doing, you bigamist? Why, dear husband, where have you been? Why are you dressed like that? What have you done with your staff? Why don't you have on your cloak?

MYRRHINA: I believe he lost it in adultery, playing lecher with Casina.

LYSIDAMUS: I'm ruined!

CHALINUS: Aren't we going to go to bed now?

[*Throws off his disguise*]

I am Casina!

LYSIDAMUS: YOU! You can go to hell!

CHALINUS [*purses lips for a kiss*]: Don't you love me?

CLEOSTRATA: Come, now, answer me! What did you do with your cloak?

LYSIDAMUS [*desperately inventing*]: It was those...those...those *women*, wife! Yes! It was a Bacchic orgy!

CLEOSTRATA: A BACCHIC ORGY!

LYSIDAMUS [*hopefully*]:   Yes, a Bacchic orgy, wife...

MYRRHINA [*intervenes*]:   He's making that up! Everyone knows the Bacchic orgies aren't playing here now.[21]

LYSIDAMUS [*aside*]:   Damn! I'd forgotten that. But still, the Bacchic orgies...

CLEOSTRATA: What about Bacchic orgies?

LYSIDAMUS: Well, if that can't happen here...

CLEOSTRATA: You're afraid they might be here?

LYSIDAMUS: *Me?* Afraid? What a lie!

CLEOSTRATA: You're awfully pale, you know.[22]

LYSIDAMUS: I'm not afraid. Why, do you think I'm lying?

CLEOSTRATA: You're asking me?

LYSIDAMUS: Myrrhina, what should I say?

MYRRHINA: You know well enough.

LYSIDAMUS: This whole business has turned out pretty rotten for me.

OLYMPIO: By the gods, I'm tickled to death to know you had such a nice time at your wedding.

LYSIDAMUS: Shut up. I'm sick and tired of this game.

OLYMPIO: You started the game, old man.

LYSIDAMUS: You think it's a *game* to make a poor old man wretched and worry him to death?

CLEOSTRATA: Now, Olympio, tell him. Go on.

OLYMPIO: You wanted to cheat me. You wanted Casina all for yourself. I see that.

LYSIDAMUS: Won't you shut up?

OLYMPIO: No, by the gods, I won't shut up! You begged me over and over to take Casina to be my wife, but only so *you* could have her.

LYSIDAMUS [*innocently*]:   *I* did that?

OLYMPIO: Oh, no, of course you didn't. It was Hector of Troy.

LYSIDAMUS: Ha! He'd have laid *you* out from the start!

[*To women, all innocence*]

Did I *really* do the things he said I did?

CLEOSTRATA: You have to ask?

LYSIDAMUS [*as if realizing the truth for the first time*]:   Well, if I did it, I was wrong.

CLEOSTRATA: Come inside the house. If your memory fails you, I'll refresh it.

LYSIDAMUS: I think I'd rather take your word for all you say.

[*Falls on his knees*]

But, wife, grant pardon to your husband.

[*Turns to Myrrhina*]

Myrrhina, plead with Cleostrata for me.

[*To company and audience*]

If I ever fall in love with Casina after this, or if I ever begin to—not to speak of making love—if I ever hereafter do anything of the sort

[*To Cleostrata*]

you'll have every right, my wife, to string me up by my thumbs and give me a sound lashing.

MYRRHINA [*eagerly*]: Oh, I think *this* pardon ought to be granted!

CLEOSTRATA [*grimly*]: I'll do as you say.

[*Turns to audience, brightly*]

And the main reason I shall grant this pardon now, and with less reluctance, is to avoid making a long play even longer than it already is.

[*Resumes her grim pose*]

LYSIDAMUS: You're not angry?

CLEOSTRATA [*grimly*]: No, I'm not angry!

LYSIDAMUS: I can take you at your word?

CLEOSTRATA: That's what I *said*!

LYSIDAMUS: Ah, no one has a more charming wife than I have!

CLEOSTRATA: Come, now.

[*To Chalinus*]

Give him back his staff and cloak.

CHALINUS: Here you are.

[*Hands them over; the company pauses; he turns to audience*]

By the gods, what a terrible wrong was done me today! I married two husbands, and neither of them treated me the way a new bride should be treated.

[*Steps forward to deliver epilogue*][23]

Dear spectators, to you I'll now confide
what next will happen when we're inside.
Casina's mystery will at last stand revealed:
she's Alcesimus's daughter, long concealed!
She'll wed Euthynicus, my master's boy.
He's handsome and young and this play's last ploy.[24]

Each man who claps till his hands are made sore
without his wife's knowledge may have any whore.
But those who refuse now to applaud,
instead of embracing some lovely young bawd
can mate with a goat whose scent has been fixed
with slime and bilge water drawn from a ditch.

[*Exeunt omnes*]

NOTES

The translation is largely based on the text and commentary of W. Thomas MacCary and M. Wilcock, *Plautus: Casina* (Cambridge, 1976).

INTRODUCTION: LUST IN ACTION

1. The prologue is more a mine of philological information than an effective introduction to the play. Prologue's comments about debased coinage and the revival of *Casina* long after Plautus's death have been taken as signs of a revival of the play anywhere from 155 B.C. to 133 B.C. See further remarks in the notes to the translation below.

2. For the earliest (and highly unfavorable) comparison of a Greek comic poet with his Roman imitator see Aulus Gellius, *The Attic Nights* (2.3), on Caecilius's adaptation of Menander's *Plokion* (*The Necklace*).

3. My interpretation of the play owes much to the commentary of MacCary and Wilcock and the illuminating analysis of Lysidamus's character by Jane M. Cody, "The *Senex Amator* in Plautus' *Casina*," *Hermes* 104 (1976): 453–476.

CASINA

1. At the most conservative estimate, lines 5–22 of the prologue (here bracketed) could be omitted, since they come from a revival of the play. The prologue can be delivered in its entirety (and has been in the production of this script), but it will be

something of a tour de force for the actor who delivers it, conveying as it does the rather complicated message that the audience is about to see (1) an English translation of (2) an ancient revival after the playwright's death of (3) a comedy of Plautus which itself was an adaptation from (4) the original Greek comedy of Diphilus. In terms of theatricality, the main objection to the prologue is that it supplies a great deal of information which only *supplements* the play with a report about Diphilus and three characters (presumably central in his comedy) who never appear in *Casina*: the young lover Euthynicus, Casina, and the slave who discovered her and who was the key to revealing her identity. Thanks to the opening scene between Chalinus and Olympio, the play's action is intelligible without the prologue; and if a trimmer script were desired, it could be cut altogether.

2. Literally, the prologue invents a festival called the Alcedonia, a celebration of halcyon days.

3. *Kleroumenoi* is Greek for "men drawing lots" (the lot-drawing occurs in II.6); *Sortientes* is its Latin translation.

4. There is a learned pun in the original which is impossible to reproduce literally: Plautus is called the poet "with a barking name" (*cum latranti nomine* [line 34]) because the Latin adjective *plautus* means "flat-eared," like a beagle.

5. The Carthaginians and the Greeks were old enemies, notorious (to the Romans at least) for treachery. Some of the people of Apulia in southern Italy (the scene of many savage campaigns during the second Punic War) defected to Hannibal; hence the added sarcastic epithets, when the memory of those wars would have still been green.

6. This line has been suspected to be an interpolation or at least out of logical sequence, since Olympio is in the middle of a detailed enumeration of Chalinus's tasks. But it plays very well. Olympio is not a bright fellow, and his ideas often tumble out in no coherent manner.

7. Cleostrata and Lysidamus both play at their roles: she at her indignation, he at his sweetness and loyalty to his wife.

8. Chalinus's poorly concealed contempt for his master is evident from the beginning of the scene. His sentence begins with *te* (*te uxor aiebat tua*, line 279 in the Latin), "you." With proper timing it should sound like an alternate object of Lysidamus's curse, *di omnes deaeque perdant* (line 279). He later employs the same kind of wit in the lot-drawing scene (II.6), where he often interrupts Olympio in mid-sentence.

9. I.e., to Lysidamus. The mythological parallels of Lysidamus as Jupiter and Cleostrata as Juno are drawn several times (in this scene, II.3, and II.6).

10. Religious and juridical ceremonies had to proceed without ill omens or errors in the ritual. The slightest slip could lead to bad luck, wrong decisions, or some other unfavorable outcome. Olympio, understandably nervous, tries to ensure that Cleostrata has not rigged the urn and lots, while Chalinus, with the opposite aim in mind, constantly seeks to ruin Olympio's prayers for victory. Olympio is similarly preoccupied in the wedding ceremony in IV.4.

11. Obscure mythological allusions are rare in Plautus. The story is that the descendants of Hercules drew lots for the districts of the Peloponnese. Cresphontes and his nephews, sons of his brother Aristodemus, were to draw lots to see who should have Messenia. Cresphontes very much wanted to win, so his crafty brother Temenus made two lots of clay, one dried in the sun for his nephew and the other baked in fire for his brother. When the nephew's lot dissolved in the water, Cresphontes won with the terra-cotta lot. The parallel is apt for the scene, but the myth cannot be entirely explained for the benefit of the audience without spoiling Olym-

pio's rejoinder to Lysidamus ("If this *scholar* here will let me"). Chalinus's line is a compromise between total obscurity and too much clarity.

12. Male and female slaves were subject to their master's pleasure, often from an early age. Plautus is not only exploiting this scene for its comic effects; confusion of sexual identity is a pervasive theme in *Casina*: Chalinus's disguise as Casina (IV.4) and Olympio's messenger speech about his experiences in the bedroom with the person he thinks is Casina (V.2).

13. Lysidamus's lines (523–524 in the Latin) are badly preserved but go something like this? "See to it that you follow the song the blackbird sings in his song: let them come 'with food or whatever,' as if they were marching to Sutrium." Sutrium was on the frontier of Latium and Etruria, and a quick march there during wars with Gauls and Etruscans led to the proverb *quasi eant Sutrium*, "As if they were going to Sutrium."

14. Alcesimus becomes quite incoherent in this scene, and his "Well nows" (*quin*) are ungrammatical and, as Lysidamus soon discovers, infectious.

15. This scene is a parody of the entrance of a heroine in high tragedy, very possibly a parody in particular of Andromache's lament in the *Andromache* of Plautus's contemporary Ennius. A fragment from that play reads:

What shall I seek for aid or refuge? Whither now
by aid of flight or exile am I borne?
Deprived am I of citadel and city!
Whence to go? Where to plead?

Pardalisca employs both the meter and the diction of tragedy, as well as highly artificial figures of speech such as anaphora, alliteration, and assonance, all of which builds up into a splendidly overdone style. Note also that she slips in and out of the tragic style as she alternately plays her role and comments on Lysidamus's reactions to her tale. For a modern audience, bad Elizabethan tragedy (convoluted sentence structure, archaisms) is the high style to play against.

16. Now Casina is made to sound like one of the Danaids: the fifty sisters who killed their own husbands on their wedding night are the women of Aeschylus's *Suppliant Women*.

17. Lysidamus commits the same indiscretion in II.6.

18. For a moment Olympio speaks in Greek, and Lysidamus answers him in kind. Unlike French words sprinkled over English, Greek words in Plautine Latin are not a sign of pretensions to elegance but indicate a lapse into the kind of colloquial language one heard on the street in the Rome of Plautus's day. Greek is always spoken by lower-class characters in Plautus, and here it underscores the absurdity of Olympio's claim to be acting in fine aristocratic style.

19. Literally "none of that barbarian fodder," *barbaricus* (from Greek *barbarikos*) being the Greeks' regular word for non-Greeks, including Romans.

20. Olympio's long scene is a rival in brilliance to the mad scene of Pardalisca (III.5) and should be played as a parody of a messenger speech in tragedy. In essence, act 5, scs. 2–4, are scenes of *anagnoresis*, or recognition, though what is discovered is Chalinus's erection.

Many of the lines in this and the following pages are corrupt or lost beyond repair, but enough remains to construct a playable finale. For a translation faithfully reflecting the many *lacunae*, see Nixon's version in the Loeb edition.

21. Myrrhina may be alluding to a decree of the senate in 186 B.C. which banned the worship of the god Bacchus inside the city of Rome.

22. From this point down to Cleostrata's command to Olympio ("Olympio, tell

him! Go on"), the assignment of the parts, like the text, is uncertain. Olympio's repudiation of his former accomplice was perhaps longer and more colorful than what remains.

23. Some doubt has been raised about the speaker of this epilogue, but the lines surely belong to Chalinus. It is typical of Plautus's stagecraft to break the dramatic illusion by having one of the principals step forward to address the audience.

24. Chalinus is alluding to the plot of the original comedy by Diphilus, which was already the object of rather cavalier treatment in Prologue's outline of its story.

TRUCULENTUS or THE SAVAGE SLAVE

THE SLAVE WHO KNEW BETTER

In Cicero's dialogue *De Senectute* (*On Old Age*), Cato the Elder explains why one should not fear old age but look forward to it as a welcome fulfillment to life. For artists there can be special rewards. Sophocles produced *Oedipus at Colonus* in his eighties. As for the Romans, exclaims Cato, "What delight did Naevius take in his *Punic War*! how Plautus delighted in *Truculentus* and *Pseudolus*!" (*De Senectute* 14). Because of this passage, *Truculentus* is customarily assigned to Plautus's old age, around the time of *Pseudolus* (definitely known to be 191 B.C.). But the precise date of the original production remains a matter of speculation; so also does the Greek comedy on which *Truculentus* is based. For readers and audiences today, the basic question raised by this often-quoted passage in Cicero is why Plautus would rejoice in *Pseudolus* and *Truculentus* together. No two plays could have less in common. *Pseudolus* is like Plautus's more popular *Menaechmi*, *Mostellaria*, and *Miles Gloriosus*. Its tone is generally sunny, and its ending cheerful. Not so *Truculentus*. Even in a theater which delights in the comic inversion of traditional values and conventional behavior, it stands out as by far the most sardonic of all Plautus's comedies.

Phronesium of Athens is in the business of making as much money as she can from her lovers. With the able assistance of her maid Astaphium and an old flame, Diniarchus, she succeeds in convincing the braggart warrior Stratophanes first that she has given birth to a baby and second that he is the father of the boy. An even easier conquest is the dim-witted country boy Strabax, son of her next-door neighbor. The boy's slave Truculentus tries to save him from ruin but fails and in the end even succumbs himself to the charms of Phronesium's house. The play ends with Strabax and Stratophanes arguing over who has given more gold to Phronesium. As she turns to go inside to her waiting lovers, Phronesium pauses to invite members of the audience to join her if they are so inclined.

Truculentus has a remarkable plot. Scene after scene illustrates Diniarchus's opening lines:

> A lover can spend his whole life learning
> yet never really learn
> how many ways there are to die for love.

The most original feature of the play is its static exposition of character. There is no development of a plot, only a relentless exposition of the jaded and the gullible.[1] What gives Truculentus its power in the theater is the cumulative effect of its scenes. When Truculentus first appears he scorns Astaphium and her charms (II.2); then a long sequence ensues in which Phronesium, with Diniarchus's aid, snares Stratophanes (II.3–II.8); then Strabax falls victim (III.1); then Truculentus, his guardian slave, succumbs (III.2); and *then*, when the audience thinks nothing more could happen, Diniarchus reenters with yet another speech in praise of Venus:

> No one has ever been born, or will be born,
> or will ever be found, to whom I'd wish better luck
> than Lady Venus! . . . (IV.1)

In performance, the effect of this delirious entrance can be explosive.

Here is the sharpest delineation in Roman comedy of specifically male folly. Plautus depicts every stage of the seduction and victimization of the customers of the clever courtesan Phronesium and her maid Astaphium, for that is what the men in this play are—a mob of gullible customers, even though each of them thinks of himself as Phronesium's only lover. Diniarchus, world-weary and urbane, is the first victim; then the rustic youth Strabax and his slave Truculentus; and finally the richest prize of all, Stratophanes, the *miles gloriosus*. At the end of the play, Diniarchus lives up only too well to the theme of his opening lines. First he leaves his own child on loan to Phronesium so that she can successfully carry off her plot to convince the soldier Stratophanes that he, Stratophanes, is the father of the child. Then, incredibly, although he has seen the plotting and treachery of Phronesium from close range, Diniarchus vows to return to her as soon as he can after a perfunctory marriage to the child's disgraced mother.

Truculentus makes exceptionally heavy demands on its actors and director. Long expository and moralizing monologues (I.1, II.1, IV.1) alternate with *cantica* (I.2, II.5, II.7) and some of the most vivid scenes in all of Plautus, such as the encounter between Stratophanes, Phronesium, and Cyamus (II.6–7) and the "mirror scenes" of Truculentus and Astaphium (II.2 and III.2). The stereotypical characters of New Comedy are present and recognizable by their eloquent or significant names, yet Plautus manipulates these stock types in unexpected ways. It is not a clever slave like Chalinus or Chrysalus who carries out the deception, but Phronesium herself. Furthermore, while Truculentus, Strabax, Cyamus, Stratophanes, and Callicles each act out their two dimensional roles in one or at most two scenes, the three central characters—Diniarchus, Phronesium, and Astaphium—are given much deeper parts. Each of them is a character we get to know very well, and, perhaps, better than we would like to.

Diniarchus's role is by far the longest and the most difficult. He provides much of the exposition of the plot and sets the tone of the drama. His endless capacity for self-deception and illogic will put a severe strain on actor (and thus audience) unless we realize that Diniarchus is not supposed to make sense:

> I'd far rather help her who wishes well for me
> than help myself. Why, I'm my own worst enemy! (II.4)

Diniarchus is at once a fellow conspirator in the plot to trick Stratophanes and a willing victim of the same women. He is "like a brother" to Phronesium and her maid Astaphium. He is no longer either a threat (through demands for sex) or a source of worry (through proposals of marriage), but only an ally in the game Phronesium plays with the two men still playing the game of sex. In effect, Diniarchus is neutered by his long contact with Phronesium.

If Diniarchus is the most pathological type of lover in the play, Phronesium is the very antithesis of love or passion. As her name implies, she is a woman coolly in control of all the action of the play, even more than her willing accomplice Astaphium. Diniarchus carefully translates *phronesis* into Latin (*sapientia*) so that the audience will not miss the significance of her name:

> . . . Phronesium,
> the courtesan who lives here in this house:
> her name is one I should learn from but don't.
> *Phronesis*, you know, is Greek for "good sense." (I.1)

She manages drink, sex, and intrigue with equal ease:

> A courtesan who can't drink and tend to her business
> is a blithering fool, a cheap clay pot;
> the rest of her body can be pickled,
> but her brain had better be dry. (IV.4)

She and Astaphium are far more intelligent than any male character in the play. Her successful charade of motherhood and childbirth reveals a woman who is completely free of every traditional role.

Still, if Phronesium and Astaphium are ruthless in their scheming and exploitation, an audience will feel little sympathy for their victims. Strabax gleefully anticipates throwing his mother and father's wealth to the "wolves" (*lupae*, which is also slang for "whores"). Stratophanes is a vainglorious fool who is denied the opportunity for that moment of self-recognition which Plautus gives to his most famous braggart warrior, Pyrgopolynices, at the end of *Miles Gloriosus*:

> Well, I see I've been tricked. That wretch Palaestrio!
> He got me into this trap! It's a fair penalty.
> If other adulterers had this kind of experience,
> there would be less adultery going on:
> they'd have more to be afraid of,
> and less appetite for affairs like this.

The one person who might be expected to be more stable is the old man Callicles (IV.3), yet he is more concerned with a reduction of his daughter's dowry to penalize Diniarchus than with the well-being of his child and grandchild. *Truculentus* reduces paternity and maternity to matters of finance. Interest, the metaphorical offspring of money, becomes more important than the literal offspring children (II.5, V.1).[2] What could be the binding love between a husband and his wife is reduced to the *negotium*, "business," of prostitution.

Only one character makes a genuine effort to resist the charms of

Phronesium and Astaphium: the slave Truculentus, who gives this Greek play its very Roman name. But his efforts are half-hearted at best. In spite of a ferocious first scene, he begins to weaken even in his first encounter with Astaphium; she predicts his downfall as soon as he is offstage (II.2). A *servus rusticus*, a country slave endowed with what the Romans liked to think of as superior country virtues, he makes an effort to save his stupid young master Strabax from himself. In the end he fails, but at least he is alive to the immorality of Phronesium's world and tries to challenge it. His is also the only character to change, and his second scene with Astaphium (III.2) marks a comic peripety in character. It is not a change for the better, as he himself acknowledges in his parting lines:

> The tavern I'm being led to specializes
> in gobbling up high fees for low service.

Truculentus is the savage slave who knew better, and *Truculentus* is a disturbing comedy by a playwright who is here at his most savage about the human comedy.

TRUCULENTUS or THE SAVAGE SLAVE

CHARACTERS

PROLOGUE

DINIARCHUS, *a young man of Athens, future son-in-law of Callicles*

ASTAPHIUM, *maid to Phronesium*

TRUCULENTUS, *a country slave of Strabax*

PHRONESIUM, *a courtesan*

STRATOPHANES, *a soldier*

CYAMUS, *a cook and servant of Diniarchus*

STRABAX, *a country youth, master of Truculentus*

CALLICLES, *an old man of Athens, father of Diniarchus's future wife*

MAID, *a slave of Callicles*

SYRA, *a slave of Phronesium*

Attendants to Phronesium, Stratophanes, Callicles, and Cyamus

[*Scene: A street in Athens with the houses of Phronesium and Strabax's father*]

PROLOGUE

It's Plautus' plea that you provide a plot
within your pretty city, please—a spot
where he can rear his Athens proud and high,
all by himself: no architects need apply.
So what's your pleasure?
                    Please don't turn me down.

What's that?

I get the finest spot in town?
Then how about a little tip off the top?
—Oh, very well, then.

I know when to stop.
Old-fashioned virtues flourish here, I see—
how fast your Roman tongues say NO to me!
Well, nothing ventured. Enough of playing with you.
I'll do the business I came here to do.
Upon this stage, then, Athens is depicted—
at least until our comedy is acted.
Phronesium lives here. She professes
the morals of our day, and our excesses.
From every lover she asks one favor,
to add another gift to what they gave her.
Prayers and robbery supplement her scheming
once she knows she has her victims dreaming.[1]
Her days are filled with whoring, extortions,
mock marriages, and fake abortions.
Her newest scheme will shock some of you, maybe:
you see, the secret weapon is. . .a baby!
The plot I'll now unfold is good and fertile,
though some details may cause your blood to curdle.
Old Callicles once sired a pretty daughter,
a virgin pure, till Diniarchus caught her:
Diniarchus, Athens' reigning pupil,
expert in all things prostitutional.
For maiden's hand he swore to ask her daddy,
but took maiden *head*; no order had he.
In real love life each side must give consent,
but Diniarchus came, and then. . .he went.
The girl conceived, making him a father,
and that good news proved really quite a bother.
Most young men will act in bona fides;
for him, that's as rare as joy in Hades.
Now he's returned, blind to her he should adore,
to see the only one he loves—his whore.
He'll loan the baby boy for good measure
to help her fleece two others of their treasure:
Stratophanes, soldier *gloriosus*,

first victim of this whorish hocus-pocus.
And then comes wealthy Strabax after him,
a youth of simple speech and wits so dim
his father guards him with a trusty
Roman slave, a beast with manners rusty.
Since he's the only man who's *compos mentis*,
we take his name and call this TRUCULENTUS.
Now enter Diniarchus with a lover's plea.
It's time for you to stay, and me to flee.

[*Exit*]

I.1

[*Enter Diniarchus, a dissipated young man with circles under his eyes*]

DINIARCHUS

A lover can spend his whole life learning
yet never really learn
how many ways there are to die for love.
Venus never renders balanced budgets,
though she's in charge of all accounts
a lover calls his own:
how many ways he's made a fool of,
how many ways he's brought to ruin,
how many prayers he needs to pray,
how much pouting,
how much petting,
how much punishment—
if you can believe it, gods—
how many lies he needs,
even when he's paid his fees!
Charge number one: a payroll every day
of the year. For that haul you'll get three nights.
Meanwhile, she adds on charges for money,
or wine, or oil, or flour
to find out whether you're generous or thrifty.

[*Warms to the subject*]

Think of a fisherman casting a net
on a fish pond. When the net hits bottom,

he gives it a little line. If a fish gets
inside, he's careful not to scare it off.
He tugs gently; sweeping first this way,
then that way, he snares the fish and finally pulls
it from the water. The same fate awaits a lover.
If he gives whenever asked,
and is generous instead of thrifty,
extra nights are tacked on,
and in the meantime he's swallowed the hook.
If he gets one undiluted dose of sex,
love juice runs through his vitals, and before he knows it,
he's lost himself and his money and credit as well.
And just let a lover have his whore
get mad at him, and he'll die two deaths:
first his money goes, then his brains.
And if another man is more her type, he's dead again.
Why, even when they get along with one another,
the lover still loses. If he spends only an
occasional night, his brains turn to soup.
If he sees her every night, he survives
well enough, but his money doesn't.
Before you can give her even one present,
she's ready to ask for a hundred others.
She's completely out of money,
her dress is an old rag,
she's bought a new maid,
there's a silver vase she must have,
or that bronze one,
or a fine carved couch,
or a trinket box some Greek made,
or anything else she can think of
that a lover should give his whore.

It's a full time job hiding how we
abuse our money, our credit, and ourselves.
God forbid our parents should learn what's going on!
If they found out and were able
to rein in our youthful passions now,
their austerity through us would enrich our posterity;
then, I guarantee, there'd be fewer whores and pimps

than there are now, and fewer bankrupts too.
As it is, pimps and whores swarm almost
as thick as flies in the heat of summer.
If you want to see them, there's no better place to look
than at the bankers' tables. Whores and pimps are there every
    day,
too many to count, really. There are
more whores at the tables than there are
weights for the bankers' scales.
What business they have there is a mystery to me,
unless they mean to keep track of the latest
interest rates—rates for credit to their customers,
just in case you thought they had any creditors.
In short, this is how we live today.

[*Slips into Roman officialese*][2]

IN THIS *GREAT* NATION OF OURS. . .

AMONG THIS *GREAT* PEOPLE. . .

THE STATE BEING AT PEACE AND AT EASE. . .

OUR ENEMIES HAVING BEEN CONQUERED. . .

[*Returns to more normal tone*]

a time when every man deserves a little love,
if he can pay for it.
Now, consider my case. Phronesium,
the courtesan who lives here in this house:
her name is one I should learn from, but don't.
Phronesis, you know, is Greek for "good sense."
I'll admit I have been an ardent suitor,
one always on the *closest* of terms with her,
terms a disaster to my bank account.
Now she's found somebody else who is
willing to pay more money than me,
a bigger fool with his money than I am.
The witch tells me he's only "a plague," "a burden,"
"a Babylonian soldier." Now this fellow is
said to be about to arrive from overseas,
and she's hatched a plot that goes like this:
She'll pretend she's just had a baby
so she can kick me out and live it up

with the soldier in regular Greek luxury.
She'll pretend that the soldier is the father of the boy.
That's why the slut needs this baby on loan.
Does she think she's tricking me?
Does she think she could keep *me* from finding out
if she really were pregnant?

[*Starts to go off; pauses, adds as afterthought*]

You see, I just got back to Athens the day before yesterday. I
was an ambassador on official business at Lemnos.

[*Astaphium enters from Phronesium's house*]

But here comes her little maid Astaphium, of all people! I've
had dealings with her too. Strictly business, of course.

[*Draws to one side*]

I.2

[*Enter Astaphium from Phronesium's house*]

ASTAPHIUM [*to servants inside*]:   Listen at our door and guard our
house's gate. No man should ever leave us heavier than he
found us. No barren hands that come to us should go off big
with gold.

[*In the manner of a blues singer*]

> *I know my men.*
> *Oh, how I know my men,*
> *the young ones*
> *best of all.*
> *Five or six will come at once,*
> *those beaming broths of . . . bores,*
> *to pay a social call,*
> *on their sweetheart whores.*

[*Brightly*]

Or so they say. Their plans *are* nicely laid!

[*Resumes*]

> *One pins a girl*
> *with kisses in a corner,*

and if they see
someone come to warn her,
they're all playing, joking,
until her guard's off guard.

[*Rapidly*]

Then it's stuffing,
and huffing,
and puffing,
and nothing left to eat in the house.
They're sausage stuffers,
and *they* are the sausage!

[*To audience*]

This is exactly what happens, and there are men here who
know me and know I never lie. To steal loot from looters like
us: what a novel, glorious thing to do! We do return the favor,
though. First the fools bring us their money, then they watch
while we count it up in piles.

DINIARCHUS [*aside, eyeing Astaphium*]: She's got a tongue like a whip,
and my scars show it. I've deposited funds there before.

ASTAPHIUM [*answering someone inside the house*]: Yes, you're right, I
just remembered! I'll bring him back with me to our house, if
he's at home.

[*Starts towards Strabax's house*]

DINIARCHUS: Wait a minute, Astaphium! Don't go yet.

ASTAPHIUM [*stops, not turning*]: Who says "Don't go"?

DINIARCHUS: Turn around and you'll find out.

ASTAPHIUM [*not turning*]: And who's there?

DINIARCHUS [*advances to her*]: Someone who wants nothing but
riches for you.

ASTAPHIUM: Give them then, if you want us to have them.

[*Not turning, she holds out her hand*]

DINIARCHUS [*does not respond*]: I'll see to it. Just look this way.

ASTAPHIUM [*still looks away*]: You're wasting my time, whoever you
are.

[*Starts to go off*]

DINIARCHUS [*stops her*]: You bitch! Wait!

ASTAPHIUM: Ah, a gentleman. And a bore.

[*Feels his empty hand; her curiosity is aroused*]

Now, could that be Diniarchus?

[*Gropes him*]

Indeed it is.

[*Turns around at last*]

DINIARCHUS: Greetings to you.

ASTAPHIUM: Likewise.

DINIARCHUS: Give me your hand and step this way.

ASTAPHIUM: Your slightest wish is like law to me.

DINIARCHUS: And how are you?

ASTAPHIUM: I am as well as the one whose hand I hold.

[*Without enthusiasm*]

Since you've been away, we'll have to have a dinner party.

DINIARCHUS: How nice, how *kind* an invitation, Astaphium.

[*Begins to fondle her*]

ASTAPHIUM [*withdrawing*]: Please. I'm on an errand for my mistress.

DINIARCHUS: By all means. But tell me . . .

ASTAPHIUM: What is it you want?

DINIARCHUS: Where are you going? Who is it? Who are you bringing here?

ASTAPHIUM: Archillis the midwife.

DINIARCHUS: Naughty, naughty! The smell of your trade follows you wherever you go. Now I've caught you in an open lie.

ASTAPHIUM: How so, if you please?

DINIARCHUS: Just then you said you were going out to bring a *him* here, not a *her* here. What was a man has now become a woman. An enchanting bit of bitchery! Tell me, then, who is this man, Astaphium? Some new lover?

ASTAPHIUM [*removes his hands*]: I think you have a lot of free time on your hands.

DINIARCHUS: Why do you think that?

ASTAPHIUM: You're free to spend your time minding other people's business, and at your own expense.

DINIARCHUS: And *you* gave me the free time to do it.

ASTAPHIUM: How so, if you please?

DINIARCHUS: I'll tell you how. I lost all my money at your house. *You*'re the ones who ran off with my business. If I had saved my money, I'd still be in *business*.

[Embraces her with a suggestive bump]

ASTAPHIUM *[escapes easily]*: Ha! Do you think you can farm the public lands of Venus or of Love and not go out of business?

DINIARCHUS: You've got it all wrong. Phronesium is the one who's farming public lands, not me. She let me pay the tax, then took my whole herd. *That*'s against the law.[3]

ASTAPHIUM: Most men who are bad at business do what you do: when they can't pay the pasture tax, they blame the tax collector.

DINIARCHUS: Since the grazing at your place didn't work out for me, I'd like a change, a little piece of land to plough, as much as you can give me.

[Feels her behind]

ASTAPHIUM *[slips away]*: We don't have any plough land here, only grassy pastures. If you want to plough, you'd better go to the boys. They're used to being ploughed. Our taxes are for *this* pasture land; their taxes are for another service.

DINIARCHUS: I know both fields well enough.

ASTAPHIUM: And that's why you have so much free time on your hands. First you failed with the boys, then with us. Tell me, whose business would you like this time?

DINIARCHUS *[reckons on his fingers]*: Let's see. You're harder to control. They tell more lies. Whatever they get they lose, with nothing left to show for it; at least when *you* get something, you eat and drink it up. In short, they're shameless, and you're of no account and proud of it.

ASTAPHIUM: You're insulting nobody but yourself, Diniarchus, certainly not us or the boys.

DINIARCHUS: And how do you arrive at that conclusion?

ASTAPHIUM: This is how: anyone who finds fault in someone else had better be sparkling clean himself. As clever as you are, you haven't a thing of ours, and we "no-accounts" have everything of yours.

DINIARCHUS [*melts, whining*]:   Oh, Astaphium, you never used to talk to me like this before. You were so polite when I had what's now in *your* house in *my* house.

ASTAPHIUM [*surveys Diniarchus up and down*]:   When a man's *alive*, you know him; when he dies, let him rest in peace. I knew you as long as you were *alive*.

DINIARCHUS [*covers his crotch*]:   You don't think I'm *dead*, do you?

ASTAPHIUM: *Please*. What could be more obvious? You were once known as the greatest lover in the world, and now you bring Phronesium nothing but complaints.

DINIARCHUS: It's all your fault. You rushed things too quickly. You should have taken your time robbing me; then I would have lasted a lot longer.

ASTAPHIUM: A lover is like an enemy town. . .

DINIARCHUS: . . . and your proof is. . .

ASTAPHIUM: . . . the sooner he can be sacked, the better it is for his mistress.

DINIARCHUS: I'll grant that. But friends and lovers aren't the same. The best friend you'll ever have is the one you've known the longest. That's a fact.

ASTAPHIUM: If he's still *alive*.

[*Goes off*]

DINIARCHUS [*desperate*]:   I'M NOT DEAD YET! I STILL OWN LAND AND HOUSES!

ASTAPHIUM [*returns*]:   Then *why on earth* are you standing in front of our house as if you were a stranger and a foreigner? Do go inside. You're no foreigner here. No man in the world is dearer to Phronesium's heart and soul than you, if you *really* do have land and houses.

DINIARCHUS [*declaiming*]

Though your tongue and speech be dipped in honey,
your hearts and deeds are sickled o'er with gall and bitter
  vinegar;
you utter sweet words with your tongue,
your hearts are filled with deeds of bitterness.[4]

[*Moved by his own eloquence, he stares into the middle distance*]

ASTAPHIUM: You dear, sweet boy. That's no way for you to talk.

People who talk that way war against themselves. They have
chastity belts for purses.

DINIARCHUS: You're as bad as ever, and as alluring too.

ASTAPHIUM: How we've waited for you to return from abroad!
How much the mistress has wanted to see you!

DINIARCHUS: Why?

ASTAPHIUM: Of all her lovers, you're the only one she loves.

DINIARCHUS [aside]: Bravo, land and houses! Your help came just
in time. Now, Astaphium . . .

ASTAPHIUM: Yes, dear.

DINIARCHUS: Is Phronesium at home now?

ASTAPHIUM: No matter what she is for others, she'll be at home for
you.

DINIARCHUS: Is she well?

ASTAPHIUM: Oh, yes, and I hope she'll be even better once she sees
you.

DINIARCHUS [strikes a pose; to audience]: Here's our greatest fault.
The moment we start to make love, we're ruined. If we're told
what we want to hear, we're fools enough to believe it, even if
it's a lie—and we aren't outraged, even though we should be.

ASTAPHIUM: Oh, tut-tut, that isn't how things are at all.

DINIARCHUS [turns back to his conversation with Astaphium]: You say
she really loves me?

ASTAPHIUM: You and you alone.

DINIARCHUS: I've heard she's had a baby.

ASTAPHIUM: Oh, Diniarchus, please hush!

DINIARCHUS: What's the matter?

ASTAPHIUM [pathetically]: The very mention of her labor sets poor
little me all atremble. You came very near to having
no . . . Phronesium.

[Brisk again]

Go inside, please, and see her. But you'll have to wait. She'll
be out soon; she was taking a bath.

DINIARCHUS: What are you saying? How could a woman who was
never pregnant have had a baby? I know her belly *very* well,
and I've seen no signs of swelling.

ASTAPHIUM: She kept it a secret. She was afraid she might not be

able to persuade you to let her keep the boy. She thought
she'd have to have an abortion and lose him.

DINIARCHUS: Then that Babylonian soldier must be the father, and
she's waiting for him now!

ASTAPHIUM: Yes, we've had a message from him which said he'd be
here soon.

[*Looks up and down the street*]

I'm surprised he hasn't arrived already.

DINIARCHUS: Shall I go in now?

ASTAPHIUM: Why not? Go as boldly as you would into your own
home. You're just one of the family now, Diniarchus.

DINIARCHUS: How soon will you return?

ASTAPHIUM: I'll be back soon. The place I'm going to isn't far away.

DINIARCHUS: Hurry back! In the meantime, I'll wait for you inside.

[*Goes into Phronesium's house*]

II.1

ASTAPHIUM

Ha-ha-ha! Peace and quiet!
The bore has gone inside!
At last I'm alone!
Now I'll freely say
what I want to say
just as it pleases *me*.

[*Advances to address audience*]

Inside at home my mistress sang a dirge,
lamenting this lover and his property.
He mortgaged his house and land as security
to pay for Love's real estate. It's true, he shares
in all my mistress's most important plots;
he's more a friend for his advice than for his *active* duty.

While he could give, he gave. Now he has nothing:
what he had, we have; what he has, we had.
The exchange is *only* human.
Fortunes have a way of changing in a flash.
Life is uncertain.

We recall when he was rich;
he knew us when we were poor.
What each of us remembers is what has *changed*.
Anyone would be a fool to be surprised at this.
If he's broke, we'll have to endure that.
He got his love from us, fair and square.
Why, it would be a *sin* for us to pity
any man who can't control his money!

A proper whore must have good teeth,
to laugh at men and flatter them;
she needs evil plans in her heart
and friendly words on her tongue.
A courtesan should be like a cactus:
any man she touches should suffer a sting, or a loss.

She should never heed a lover's pleas.
When he pays nothing, she should send him home for
desertion in the ranks. No man can be an honest lover
unless he's his own money's worst enemy.
The man who's best loved in our house is
the one who forgets that he has given.
As long as he has it, he can have *it*;
once he doesn't have it, let him get *it*
somewhere else. When he doesn't have it,
he ought to be sensible and make way for one who does.
He gives you only trifles unless he wants to give again.
The best kind of lover at our house is the one
who first drops his affairs, and then his fortune.

Yet men are always saying to each other
that *we* do all the wrong, *we*'re the greedy ones.
Why so? I ask you, what wrong do we really do?
No, the truth is that no lover ever gives
enough to his mistress; none of us
ever gets enough, none of us ever asks enough.

Now, when a lover comes with hands barren of gifts,[5]
if he swears he has no gifts to give,
we believe him; we take no deposit from him

when he has no deposits left to give.
We always look out for new depositors,
ones who have untouched treasures.
Take the country boy who lives here.

[*Indicates the house of Strabax*]

Goodness, what a charmer, and only too ready to pay!
But his slave is a raging monster.
When he sees one of us here, he chases us
as if he were driving geese from a granary.
He's so. . . so *rural.*
But I'll give a knock, no matter whan happens.
Yoo-hoo! Is anyone in charge of this door? Is anyone here?

[*Knocks vigorously*]

II.2

TRUCULENTUS [*enters raging, with a hoe*]

Who's battering at our door? Are you a ram, or what?

[*Charges past Astaphium; looks around the stage*]

ASTAPHIUM [*behind him*]:   Just me. Do turn around.
TRUCULENTUS [*over shoulder*]:   Who's "me"?
ASTAPHIUM: Don't I look like me to you?
TRUCULENTUS [*turns*]:   You! Why did you come here? Why did you
    try to beat our door down?
ASTAPHIUM: Good health to you.
TRUCULENTUS: Enough of your "good health." Don't need it. Not
    healthy anyway. Rather be sick than healthy with your "good
    health." What I want to do know is, WHAT'S YOUR BUSINESS
    WITH THIS HOUSE?
ASTAPHIUM: For the sake of your mistress, calm down!
TRUCULENTUS: Make her *come*, did you say? That's your style, eh.
    You want to make me make our *mistress* come?[6] You have no
    shame, trying to trick an honest country man into taking a
    tumble.
ASTAPHIUM: But I only said "calm down" for your mistress's sake.
    You took *l* out of the word when you heard it.

[*Aside*]

And then took *l* out on me. This creature is too truculent for
words.

TRUCULENTUS [*raising his hoe as if to strike her*]:   What! More of your
insults, is it . . . you . . . you . . . *woman*, you?

ASTAPHIUM: Insults? What insults?

TRUCULENTUS: Saying I'm succulent, that's what.[7]

[*She begins to protest, but he silences her*]

Now, look here, woman, if you don't clear out of here at once
or tell me what I want to know, then *damned* if I don't stomp
you under my foot like a sow stomps a litter.

ASTAPHIUM [*to audience*]:   That one came straight off the farm.

TRUCULENTUS [*bellows with rage*]:   You chattering tribe of monkeys!
You're a disgrace, that's what you are!

[*She walks seductively towards him; for a moment he watches her,
mesmerized*]

You came here to show yourself off, didn't you? Every limb
covered with trinkets. I'll bet you dyed that rag of a dress by
holding it over some campfire.

[*She approaches closer*]

You think you're pretty because you've got these bronze
bracelets!

ASTAPHIUM [*against him, twirling her fingers in his hair*]:   You're cute
when you curse like that.

TRUCULENTUS [*tries to remain oblivious to her actions*]:   Then try this
one on for size. You think that if you wear that cheap paste
you'll be a high-class lady? I'll bet those jewels hanging from
your ears are fake.

[*Snatches at an earring*]

ASTAPHIUM [*yanks his hand away and places it around her waist*]:   Don't
you lay a finger on me!

TRUCULENTUS: *Me* finger *you*? Ha! By this trusty little hoe, I swear
I'd rather be off in the country embracing some broad-
beamed cow. I'd rather spend every night of my life in the
straw with her than eat at your place for a hundred.

[*Astaphium is very busy with his hair, ears, etc.; her success is shown by the trembling of the hoe*]

So it's a disgrace to come from the country? Well, you've met one man who thinks it's a disgrace to do what you do. What's your business with this house, you...you...*woman*, you? Why do you come here every time we come to town?

ASTAPHIUM [*rearranging herself*]:   I want to meet the women of the house.

TRUCULENTUS: You talk to me of women when there's not so much as a female fly inside these doors?

ASTAPHIUM: What? No women at all live here with you?

[*Moves in closer*]

TRUCULENTUS: THEY'VE GONE OFF TO THE COUNTRY, I TELL YOU! GET OUT!

ASTAPHIUM: Why are you shouting so, you silly boy?

[*Locks her arms around him and presses close*]

TRUCULENTUS [*realizing what she is doing, he frees himself and holds her off with his hoe*]:   If you don't hustle yourself out of here in double time, I'll yank those false, dainty, frizzled, frilled, perfumed locks out by the roots, brains and all!

[*Pushes her away*]

ASTAPHIUM [*plays the helpless female*]:   Whatever for?

TRUCULENTUS: Because you dared to come near this house, because you drip with perfume, because you were shameless enough to color your cheeks with...with...

[*Weakens slightly*]

with such a pretty little ruby tint.

ASTAPHIUM [*the innocent virgin*]:   Oh dear, I swear I blushed red because of your terrible shouting...poor thing that I am.

TRUCULENTUS [*examines her cheeks closely*]:   You blushed yourself red, did you? As if there were a single part of your body that could show any more color.

[*She snuggles up to him; he jumps back*]

You witch! You've painted your cheeks with red paint and your body with white powder. You're the worst women alive!

ASTAPHIUM: And what harm have the most wicked women in the world done you?

TRUCULENTUS [*draws himself together*]:   I know more than you think I know.

ASTAPHIUM: And what might it be that you know?

TRUCULENTUS [*raging again*]:   I know our master's son Strabax is being ruined in your house. You're ruining him, snaring him in your wicked schemes and scandals.

ASTAPHIUM: If I believed you were in your right mind, I'd say you were slandering me. As it is, no men are ever ruined in our house the way you say. Why, there's no need for us to assist them at all! Each one is able to ruin himself quite nicely—and, I might add, quite unaided. After they've spent everything they have, they're welcome to depart whenever they wish.

[*With renewed interest*]

I don't believe I've had the pleasure of meeting this young man of yours.

TRUCULENTUS: Is that so? What about that wall that separates your garden patch from ours? It gets lower and lower every night as he walks through on the road to his ruination.

ASTAPHIUM [*fiddling with her jewelry, coyly*]:   That's not strange at all. The mortar is old.

[*Suggestively*]

All old garden walls fall down eventually.

TRUCULENTUS [*follows her eyes and immediately covers his crotch*]:   So! That's your line, eh? "Old garden walls fall down"! I'm going to denounce your scheme to the boy's father! If I don't, may no mortal soul ever trust my oaths or prayers again!

ASTAPHIUM: Is he as foul-tempered as you?

TRUCULENTUS [*without realizing it, Astaphium takes his hoe and leans on it, listening intently to his tirade*]:   You can be sure of one thing: he doesn't spend his money to keep cheap whores in luxury. He uses it in thrifty, hard-headed ways. And it's his money that's being exported in secret to your house! Damn you! You gobble it down, spray it on, drink it up! You think I'll keep my mouth shut about all this? No. I'm going to the forum right now to tell the boy's father everything I know. This back is one field that will never know a whip's furrows.

[*Stalks off down the street. Immediately on exiting, he realizes that he has left his hoe. He comes back, snatches it from Astaphium, and leaves again*]

ASTAPHIUM [*to audience*]:   If that fellow had been fed on nothing but a diet of mustard seed he couldn't be more sour. Too tart even for me! My goodness, he does live only for his master, doesn't he? All the same, I hope to change his ways with flattering words, abject prayers, and all the other tricks we courtesans use. I've seen wild horses tamed who never thought to yield; the same thing can happen to other *beasts* as well.

[*Fusses with her hair and jewels*]

I'll look in a bit on my mistress now.

[*Diniarchus enters*]

Oh dear, here comes my burden back again. But how subdued! He must not have met with Phronesium yet.

II.3

DINIARCHUS [*despondently*]:   I'm sure that fish who pass their entire lives in water don't bathe as much as that Phronesium. If women spent as much time making love as they spend taking baths, all their lovers would have to serve double time as bath attendants.

ASTAPHIUM: What's so *hard* about having to wait a little while?

DINIARCHUS: I'll tell you what's *hard*! Waiting is what's *hard*! I'm so tired now I need a bath myself. Please, Astaphium, go inside and say that I'm here. Get her to hurry on out here! She's bathed enough.

ASTAPHIUM: Very well.

[*Starts to go in*]

DINIARCHUS: Oh, listen. . .

ASTAPHIUM: What is it?

DINIARCHUS: May the gods curse me for calling you back! Didn't I just tell you to go?

ASTAPHIUM: Then *why* did you call me back, you worthless fool! You've made a mile's worth of delay for yourself.

[*Exit*]

DINIARCHUS [*to audience*]: But why did she stand here so long in front of their house? She's on the lookout for somebody. I'll bet it's that soldier. Yes, *he*'s the one they're after! They're like vultures: they see three days ahead of time when they're going to have a good meal. He's the one they're gaping for! He's the one on their minds! The minute he arrives they'll pay no more attention to me than if I'd been dead for two hundred years. How nice it must be to save your money! Too bad for me. I've reformed after the fact. I've aborted the goods my parents gave birth to. If I could somehow get my hands on one more inheritance, a great big juicy one, now that I know the sweet and the bitter things that money brings, I'd save every penny. I'd be so stingy from one day to the next, why . . . why

[*Ruefully*]

inside a few days, I'd have it down to nothing. Yes, that's how I'd show those carping critics of mine.

[*The door to Phronesium's house opens*]

Ah, that steaming hot door is opening, the one that gobbles up everything that passes through it!

II.4

[*Phronesium appears at her door with two servants; she drapes herself seductively on the threshold*]

PHRONESIUM: Why, dear, you don't think my *door* will bite, do you? Is that why you're afraid to come inside, darling?

DINIARCHUS [*transported*][8]

Ah, behold, the spring . . .

she blooms . . .

perfumes . . .

her eyes . . .

breed sighs.

PHRONESIUM [*advances, followed by servants*]: Why are you so rude, Diniarchus? Here you are returned from Lemnos, and not one kiss for your mistress?

DINIARCHUS: Ahhhhh! I'm in for a terrible beating now!

[*Trying to escape, he turns to go*]

PHRONESIUM: Why did you turn away?

DINIARCHUS [*returns*]: Greetings to you, Phronesium.

PHRONESIUM: And to you. You'll have dinner with us, won't you, now that you're back safe and sound?

DINIARCHUS [*tries to escape*]: I'm already spoken for.

PHRONESIUM: Where might that be?

DINIARCHUS [*collapses*]: Wherever you say.

PHRONESIUM: Then here. Dine with us and make me happy.

DINIARCHUS: And me happier still. You mean you'll spend the whole day with me, my Phronesium?

PHRONESIUM: I would if it were possible.

DINIARCHUS [*as if already in the dining room, to an imaginary slave*]: Here! Put these sandals on! Hurry up! Get the dining table out of here!

PHRONESIUM [*alarmed*]: Oh dear, are you all right?

DINIARCHUS [*reeling*]: No, I can't drink now. I feel so faint.

[*Staggers about the stage*]

PHRONESIUM: Wait, don't go off! We'll find some way to work things out.

DINIARCHUS [*comes to momentarily*]: Ah, your words have revived me like a drink of cool water. I feel better already.

[*Again transported to his imaginary dining room*]

My sandals! Take them off! Give me a drink!

PHRONESIUM [*smiles*]: You're your old self again, I see. But tell me, how did you enjoy your little trip abroad?

DINIARCHUS: Any trip that brought me back to you would be a pleasant one. Just *seeing* you is reward enough.

PHRONESIUM [*in a perfunctory manner*]: Embrace me.

DINIARCHUS: Gladly. Oh, this is sweeter than the sweetest honey. Jupiter, now I'm luckier in love than even you!

PHRONESIUM [*as flatly as before*]: Kiss me.

DINIARCHUS: Not once but ten times!

PHRONESIUM [*backing away*]: There, see why you're poor? You're always promising more than I ask from you.

DINIARCHUS: I only wish that you had been as sparing of my money as you are now of your kisses.

PHRONESIUM: If I could possibly save you anything, I would.

DINIARCHUS: All finished with your bath now?

PHRONESIUM: Why, yes, I am, so far as I can tell. You don't think I'm *dirty*, do you?

DINIARCHUS: Oh, no, of course *I* don't. There was a time when we didn't mind it if we both got dirty. Now I'm back. What new plot have you hatched while I was gone?

PHRONESIUM: What do you mean?

DINIARCHUS [*sarcastically*]:   Well, first of all, congratulations on your growing family. I'm glad you passed through that ordeal so well.

PHRONESIUM [*to her servants*]:   Go back inside and shut the door, girls.

[*They go inside*]

Now you and you alone shall hear what I have to say. I'm entrusting all my most secret plans to you. The fact is that I didn't have a baby boy. The fact is I wasn't even pregnant. I did pretend to be pregnant, I can't deny that.

DINIARCHUS: Whom did you do that for, light of my life?

PHRONESIUM: For that Babylonian soldier. He kept me like a wife the year he lived here.

DINIARCHUS: That's what I thought happened. But why did you? What good was all that pretending?

PHRONESIUM: To make a little bond, a tie to guarantee he'd come back to me. Not too long ago he sent a letter saying he'd return to find out just how much I cared for him; if I didn't kill the child I'd had, but brought it up, he'd give me everything he owned.

DINIARCHUS: Do continue. I'm all ears. What happened next?

PHRONESIUM: Now that the ninth month has passed, my mother told her maids to go looking here and there, and to find a baby boy or girl that could be passed off as mine. Not to go on too long about it: you know our hairdresser Syra, the girl who lives with us?

DINIARCHUS: Yes. What has she to do with you?

PHRONESIUM: Well, her work takes her from one house to the next, so she kept her eyes open for a boy and brought one to me in secret. She *said* someone gave it to her.

DINIARCHUS: What witchery! The baby wasn't born to the mother who first bore him, but to you by a second birth.

PHRONESIUM: You've got it all in the right order. Now, according to the soldier's letter, it won't be too long before he gets here.

DINIARCHUS: And in the meantime you're going to see to it that you look like you've just had a baby?

PHRONESIUM: Why not? especially when it can be managed so easily without the labor. As the saying goes, "Everyone is best at what they do best." I'm best at this.

DINIARCHUS: But what will happen to me once the soldier comes? You think I can live without you?

PHRONESIUM: When I get from him what I want from him, I'll have no trouble finding ways to cause discord and divorce at home. After that, my love, I promise to abide by you forever.

DINIARCHUS: I'd rather have you in a *bed* by me forever!

PHRONESIUM [*ignores his meaning*]: Now a sacrifice is due the gods. It's required five days after a baby's birth.

DINIARCHUS: Of course.

PHRONESIUM: So, will you give me some little present?

DINIARCHUS: Oh, my love, I think I grow richer every time you ask me for anything!

PHRONESIUM: I feel the same way, too, once I get it.

DINIARCHUS: I'll see to it right away. I'll have my little slave Cyamus come at once.

PHRONESIUM: Yes, do just that.

DINIARCHUS: I hope you'll like whatever he brings.

PHRONESIUM: I'm sure you'll have no cause to regret anything you send me.

DINIARCHUS: There's something more you want?

PHRONESIUM: Only that you come back when you have a free moment—and that you fare well.

[*Phronesium sails into house*]

DINIARCHUS: Farewell.

[*Solo Diniarchus*]

DINIARCHUS: By the immortal gods, for her to do what she's just done was not the act of a faithful, loving woman! She's a trusting comrade whose heart's the same as mine! To confide in *me* that she had borrowed that baby boy! That's something not even one *sister* would do for another! Now that she's revealed to me her inner thoughts, I know she'll never be unfaithful as long as she lives. How could I not love her? How could I not wish her well? I'd sooner stop loving myself than leave off loving her. How could I not send her a present? I'll order Cyamus to see that she receives five minas of gold at once, and one more mina for food, at least that much!

[*Goes; pauses*]

I'd rather help her who wishes well for me
than help myself. Why, I'm my own worst enemy!

[*Brightly, exit*]

II.5

[*Enter Phronesium in dressing gown; her servants carry a crib and baby*]

PHRONESIUM [*matter-of-factly, handing the baby over to an attendant*]: Nurse this baby.

[*Begins a lyric lament*]

Oh, how wretched are we mothers,
Oh what cares upon our hearts do weigh,
Oh the tortures that we suffer . . .

[*Breaks to confide to audience, rapidly*]

Why, what an awful fabrication!
When I stop to think of it,
all we girls are known too well
for our clever wicked ways—
or should I say too slightly?
Everything I talk about
I first learned at home.

[*Reclines; resumes lament*]

Oh what worry for the spirit,
Oh what heartache to support . . .

[*Breaks again, rapidly addressing audience*]

To avoid a nasty headache, that is:
the baby's death would spoil my sport.

And since I'm called his mother,
I'm all the more eager that he live.
Now that I've dared this first part of the plot,
I'll now take up the other.
Because of money I am greedy and live
in scandal. I'll even adopt another
woman's labor as my own! Still,
it never pays to undertake an
underhanded matter unless you do it
with pride in your profession.

[*Rises from couch and addresses audience*]

See for yourselves
how properly I'm dressed: I mean to look
as though I've just given birth.
No matter what evil a woman undertakes,
if she doesn't finish it,
it makes her sick,
it makes her sad,
it makes her miserable
in her misery.
If she starts to do anything good,
very soon she comes to hate it.
Far too few of us grow tired of evil-doing
once we start it; even fewer of us
can finish a good deed once it's begun.
Evil-doing is a burden we bear
far better than doing good. I owe
my badness to my mother's training,
and no little to myself. That's why
I can pretend to be pregnant by a
Babylonian soldier. Now I want
that soldier to discover just how
carefully contrived my badness can be.
He should be arriving any moment.
I'm already set for him and made up
so I'll look sick and confined to my bed.

[*To servants*]

Put some myrrh and offerings on the altar

to honor Lucina, dear goddess
who presided at my child's birth.

[*Sharply to servants*]

Now put that down and get out of my sight!

[*Returns to the weakened tone of her lament*]

> *Oh Pithecium, help me lie down.*
> *Come help me. Ah, that's the way to treat*
> *a new mother. Take off*
> *my sandals. A cloak for me, Archillis.*
> *Where are you, Astaphium? Bring*
> *rosemary and fruit for my confinement.*
> *Some water for my hands . . .*

[*In a determined tone*]

Now, by god, I'm ready for that soldier to appear!

II.6

[*A grand pause. Then Stratophanes enters in triumphal procession. He is preceded by dancing girls, drummers, and slaves bearing spoils and trophies. At a signal from him, the dancing and chanting cease and his scribe takes up his position at the warrior's elbow. Throughout the scene the scribe tries to take down Stratophanes' more eloquent lines*]

STRATOPHANES [*addresses the audience; his gestures and delivery are those of an orator and statesman*]

Expect me not, spectators, to declaim my deeds.
It is my way to make my valor known by these hands.
I have no need of empty words.
I know that the very mention of the military
brings to mind nothing but thoughts of their mendacity.
I know that those who would boast
of exploits equal to the deeds of warriors
immortalized in Homer stand condemned
for fighting battles that never were.

[*Warming to his subject, he is increasingly oblivious of others*]

I have no use for a man who is praised
more by those who hear about his deeds

than by those who have actually seen them.
One eye-balled witness is worth more
than ten whose ears bring them report.
Those who hear things can tell
only what they have heard;
those who see know the truth firsthand.

[*Cheers from the retinue. The scribe has fallen asleep. Stratophanes wakes him with a sharp kick, whereupon he begins to write feverishly. Only after the scribe signals that he has caught up does Stratophanes continue his discourse*]

I have no use for any man whom fops in town greet
with praise while veterans keep silent in his presence;
nor for him who utters words
in the safety of his home which outdazzle real swords
in the line of battle. Men of action are worth
far more to their people than your clever,
scheming types. Valor easily finds
a moving eloquence all its own.

[*The scribe has dozed again, but before the kick lands, he jumps back, writing all the while. Stratophanes regains his balance and continues as if nothing has happened*]

I regard your citizen who is clever
but lacking in courage as a hired female mourner:
she knows how to praise others well enough,
but in truth cannot praise herself.

[*The entire procession is asleep, some leaning on their instruments, some on each other; a few are prone and audibly snoring. He awakens them by a loud clearing of his throat. They applaud vigorously and exit with ad libs about his bravery, eloquence, etc. The last to exit hurries back to snatch the scribe away just as another kick is aimed at him. He is dragged off writing furiously. Stratophanes turns the incomplete kick into a grand gesture and continues*]

Now after nine months, I've come back to
Attic Athens to see what my dear girl—
she whom I left filled with the potency
of my manly embrace—is up to.

[*He strides up and down posturing, rehearsing speech, etc.*]

PHRONESIUM: See who is talking about us so nearby.

ASTAPHIUM [*looking towards center stage, where Stratophanes is pantomiming the speech he will deliver*]: Your Stratophanes is here, Phronesium. It's time for you to start looking sick.

PHRONESIUM: Hush! Do you think you can teach me anything about plotting? I taught you everything you know.

[*Pinches baby: sound of a baby crying*]

STRATOPHANES [*brightly, to audience*]: The woman seems to have had a baby!

ASTAPHIUM: Do you want me to approach him?

PHRONESIUM: Yes.

[*During the following exchange, Astaphium blocks Stratophanes' view of Phronesium, who is busy arranging her garments and the couch for her sickbed scene*]

STRATOPHANES: Ah, excellent! Astaphium comes to meet me.

ASTAPHIUM [*with a formal salute*]: Hail to thee, Stratophanes! You're looking well.

STRATOPHANES [*returns salute*]: Yes, I know. But tell me, has Phronesium given birth?

ASTAPHIUM: She has, and to a boy that's too sweet for words.

STRATOPHANES: Ahhhh! And is he anything like me?

ASTAPHIUM: You have to ask? Why, the instant he was born he was asking for a sword and shield.

STRATOPHANES: That's proof enough for me. He's my boy.

ASTAPHIUM: He's only too much like you.

STRATOPHANES: Ah, marvelous! Is he big now? Has he served in a legion yet? What sort of spoils did he get?

ASTAPHIUM: He was born only *five* days ago!

STRATOPHANES [*anxious*]: Well, what *happened* then? With all that time on his hands he should have done *something*! What disaster could have befallen him so soon after he left his mother's womb?

ASTAPHIUM [*silently appeals to audience to witness this stupidity; shrugs*]: Follow me and greet your wife. Give her your thanks.

STRATOPHANES: I come.

[*Strikes a noble attitude and follows her to Phronesium's couch*]

PHRONESIUM [*weakly, in the style of the mother's lament*]

> *Where is the maid*
> *who left me just now, I pray?*
> *Where is she?*
> *Where has she gone?*

ASTAPHIUM: Here I am. I bring you the Stratophanes you've so longed to see.

PHRONESIUM [*half rising; her weakened eyes cannot focus*]
> *Where...is...he?*

STRATOPHANES [*grandiloquently*]
> Mars, returning from abroad, sends greetings
> to his wife, the fair nymph Neriene.

[*Phronesium and Astaphium look at one another, then at the audience, in disbelief*]

> Since you have managed all affairs in proper fashion,
> since you have increased our estate with child,
> since you have given birth to a thing of great credit
> to me...oh, yes, *and* to you...congratulations!

[*Salutes*]

PHRONESIUM [*salutes weakly, then falls back*]
> *Oh hail to thee! Thrice welcome, you who nearly*
> *deprived me of life and limb. You had your fun,*
> *then left me with something that has ruined*
> *my health and left me with a sickness unto death.*

[*Rises, then falls back again*]

STRATOPHANES: Tut-tut, my beloved, this labor has not befallen you unrewarded. You've given birth to a son who will fill your home with spoils.

PHRONESIUM: We stand in much greater need of having our storehouses filled with grain! We'll be long dead from hunger before *he* wins any spoils.

STRATOPHANES: Be of good cheer.

PHRONESIUM [*tries to rise; falls back*]
> *Give me a kiss. Ah! I cannot lift my head...*
> *the pain is too great. I cannot walk without your help.*

STRATOPHANES [*lifting her awkwardly from the couch*]: If you ordered me to come to your embrace in the middle of the sea, I swear I would plunge straight in, my honeybuns.

[Everyone winces]

You know that well enough.

[He places her next to the pile of gifts his servants have left]

Now, my dear Phronesium, you will see the proofs of my love for you. Behold my gifts to you! I've brought you two serving maids from Syria.

[He claps his hands and motions to attendants]

You there, bring them here. Both came from a royal house. I should know. I laid waste the entire country.

[Scribe brings two young women forward and delivers them to Astaphium; Phronesium does not even look at them]

This is my gift to you.

PHRONESIUM: Aren't you ashamed, when I already have too many servants to feed? Now you bring me still more to gobble up my groceries?

STRATOPHANES *[in disbelief, aside]*: The gift is not a welcome one! You, boy, hand me that little sack there. My best beloved, behold: I bring this cloak to you from Phrygia!

PHRONESIUM *[glances at a magnificent robe disdainfully and hands it to Astaphium]*: This teeny-tiny thing? Is this all I get for my labors?

STRATOPHANES *[aside]*: As, wretch that I am, I am undone! My son is costing me his weight in gold! And it didn't matter that the cloak was made of royal purple.

[To Phronesium]

From Arabia I bring frankincense; from the Black Sea, balsam. They're all yours, my delight.

PHRONESIUM: I'll take them.

[Hands them to Astaphium without so much as a look]

Astaphium, get these *trinkets* and *Syrians* out of my sight.

[Exeunt Astaphium and scribe with young women]

STRATOPHANES: Now do you love me?

PHRONESIUM: Not a bit. You haven't earned anything at all.

STRATOPHANES: Will nothing satisfy you?

[*Aside, to audience*]

> She hasn't said one friendly word to me. I'll bet she could get twenty minas for the gifts I've given her. She seems angry now.

[*Looks at her; Phronesium quickly puts on her best scowl*]

> Remarkable! Yes, she's plainly angry. Then I'll be off.

[*He starts off, but noticing that she has not noticed, comes back*]

> Now, what would you say if I were to invite myself to dinner, my delight? I'll come back then for the night.

[*Phronesium ignores him*]

> Why are you so quiet?

[*Aside*]

> I'm done for!

[*Phronesium returns to her couch and weakly turns her face away from him; she is a study in tragedy and suffering. Suddenly there are distant sounds of Cyamus's parade*]

> But what's this strange sight? Who is that fellow leading this parade? I'll take up a sentry post here and watch what they do. They're bringing something in to her. Whatever it is, I'll know soon enough.

[*Stands off to one side, with insufferable dignity*]

II.7

[*Enter Cyamus with a train of servants carrying food, wine, etc. They dance merrily to the rhythm of his opening lines*]

CYAMUS

> *This way, this way, step over here,*
> *you ambulating asses with a fool for a master!*
> *You housecleaning harpies breeding doom and disaster!*
> *The only thing you're good for is carrying out the loot!*

[*They ignore him and continue dancing. He turns to the audience*]

Can a man in love be anything but a zero?
A man who turns his purse inside-out
to pursue the not-so-fine art of whore-mongering?
Does anybody here need to ask
why I know the answer to these questions?
Well, we've got a lover at home who lunges
from one scandal to the next. He treats
his property like so much dung:
"Take it out! Take it out!"
that's his command.
Maybe he's afraid of fleas?
The place is spotless!

[*Chuckles*]

He wants a clean house, and we see to *that* well enough. Everything inside gets carried outside! Since Diniarchus's passion is to ruin himself with passion, I see no harm in helping him—discreetly, of course. He would race to his doom soon enough without help from anyone, but just to speed him on his way, I drag one drachma off every ten he gives me for the groceries. Accounts deceivable, so to speak.

[*Raises his arms to heaven*]

Oh great Hercules!

[*Sings*]

Your tithe
is my tithe.

[*Signals to his followers*]

If you want to understand what is going on, picture a raging flood. If a man should redirect some of that great torrent of water onto his own fields, what's the harm in that? If the water weren't channeled off, it would all run out to sea anyway. That's a fact. This stuff

[*Points to the provisions*]

is running out to sea, to a miserable, rotten end! When I see such things going on

[Rhythmic chant is cheerleaderlike]

I embezzle!

ATTENDANTS

Yeah!

CYAMUS

I bamboozle!

ATTENDANTS

Yeah!

CYAMUS

I deboot them
of their booty,

ATTENDANTS

Yeah!

CYAMUS

because. . .

[He and his attendants sing and form a chorus line]

A whore and the ocean are much the same.
Way we see it, just a difference in name.
Give what you got, 'cause they won't overflow.
Just stick it all in, no limit they know.

[Addresses audience again]

I'll say this much, though:
whatever you do sink in
stays well hidden.

[Sings again]

Give all you want, you won't see it again.
It stays in the lady on the other end.

[Rapidly]

That's what happened to my poor master when a whore
brought him straight to the door of disaster. She stripped him
of property, life, reputation, friends. . .

[At last he comes to his senses; notices Phronesium]

Say! Speaking of strippers, there she is now! I'll bet she's
heard everything I said.

[Puzzled]

Why, she's pale, as if she had just given birth to a baby boy.

[Brightly, aside]

I'll address her as if I knew nothing.

[To Phronesium and Astaphium]

I earnestly desire your good health, ladies.

PHRONESIUM: Ah, Cyamus, my dear, what are you up to? How are things? You're well, I hope?

CYAMUS: I am well. I come to one who's not so well, but I bear something that will make her more...well.

[Grand gesture]

My master, that little apple of your eye,

[Indicates his own eye]

has ordered me to bring you the gifts borne by these slaves.

[Phronesium reacts, but he stops her with upraised hand and purse]

Here also are five minas of silver.

PHRONESIUM *[showing the purse to Astaphium and cooing]*: Oh, by the gods, is it any wonder that I love Diniarchus so!

[Stratophanes groans audibly and while following the conversation appeals to the audience to witness such treachery]

CYAMUS: He also commands me to beg that these gifts will please you.

PHRONESIUM: They *do* please me, they are so welcome! Now, Cyamus, please be a dear and have these fellows take everything inside.

CYAMUS *[to his servants, clapping his hands]*: Didn't you hear the lady's orders? Get to it! I don't want these wine jugs carted off, so tell the slaves inside to pour the wine into empty jugs and return these to me.

PHRONESIUM: Why, Cyamus! How presumptuous of you!

CYAMUS: Me?

PHRONESIUM: You.

CYAMUS: Oh, really! You call *me* presumptuous when you yourself are a stable of vices?

PHRONESIUM [*begins to respond but decides not to lower herself; smiles*]: Tell me, where is my darling Diniarchus?

CYAMUS: At home.

PHRONESIUM: Inform him that because of the gifts he has sent me, I now love him more than any other man in the world. Tell him that I hold him in the very *highest* esteem and that I yearn for him to come to me.

[*Stratophanes roars in agony and rage; gnaws at his knuckles*]

CYAMUS [*perfunctorily*]: As you say.

[*Notices Stratophanes for the first time*]

Who is that fellow over there chomping on himself?

[*Phronesium shrugs as if she does not know*]

That miserable looking one with the evil eye. He's in a foul mood, whoever he is.

PHRONESIUM [*as if seeing Stratophanes for the first time*]: Yes, and he deserves every bit of it. He's worthless.

[*Cyamus moves towards Stratophanes*]

Look carefully, don't you recognize him?

[*Cyamus looks more closely. Stratophanes is frozen in rage, his fist stuffed in his mouth*]

He's the soldier who used to live in my house. He's the father of this little boy here. I've driven him off,

[*Cyamus pushes Stratophanes*]

and still he stays around, listening and observing everything I do.

CYAMUS: I know the worthless fellow. Is that him?

[*He stands eyeball to eyeball with Stratophanes*]

PHRONESIUM: Yes, that's him.

CYAMUS [*Stratophanes groans*]: He moans at me! He glares at me!

[*Another growl from Stratophanes*]

That sigh was wrenched from the very bottom of his belly!

[*Stratophanes begins to pound on his thighs in impotent rage*]

And look at this! He's gnashing his teeth like a charging horse! He's slapping his thigh.

[*A thundering roar; Cyamus runs over to Phronesium*]

Is he a soothsayer beating himself into a frenzy?

STRATOPHANES [*explodes at last*]

NOW shall I unleash the raging spirits
and the smoldering wrath that bubbles and boils
in my bosom! How dare you address such rude words to me?
ME!

CYAMUS [*mildly*]

Passing fancy.

STRATOPHANES

Don't you dare talk to me that way!

CYAMUS

Then try this way: I don't give a damn who you are.

STRATOPHANES [*to Phronesium*]

And what about you? How dare you say you love another man?

PHRONESIUM

Passing fancy.

[*She walks away and with Astaphium begins an inventory of the gifts*]

STRATOPHANES

Oh, is that so?

[*Aside*]

I'll test that little remark first.

[*To Phronesium*]

Do you mean to tell me that for the sake
of such trivial gifts as these vegetables,
these scraps of food,
this vinegar water we drink on campaigns,
that for all this you've fallen in love with a
DIMPLE-ASSED GIGOLO?
A PILE OF CURLY HAIR?
A MILKY-WHITE FROM INDOOR SPORTS?

A MERE TAMBOURINE THUMPER?

LESS THAN A MAN?

NOT EVEN A MOUSE?

[*Phronesium neither looks up nor acknowledges his anger, only nods yes*]

CYAMUS: Now, just a minute there! You shameless wretch, you fountain of iniquity and lies, do you dare speak ill of *my* master?

STRATOPHANES: Add one more word to that list, and damned if I don't take this sword and hack you into hamburger!

CYAMUS: You lay one hand on me and I'll split you down the middle like a lamb ready for the roasting pit!

[*Draws kitchen knife*]

You may be a great warrior in the legions, but around here the king of the kitchen is me!

PHRONESIUM [*looking up calmly from her examination of the gifts, to Stratophanes*]: If you had any sense of fair play, you wouldn't attack my guests so viciously. After all, everything I got from him was fine and welcome; everything I got from you was worthless.

STRATOPHANES: Then, by the gods, am I stripped now of life and property alike!

PHRONESIUM: Well, of course you are.

CYAMUS: Why do you keep hanging around her when all your efforts lead to nothing? What a bore.

[*Begins to trim nails with his knife*]

STRATOPHANES [*exasperated*]: Now, by the gods, may I perish this very day if I don't drive this beggar away from you!

CYAMUS: Ha! Come on! Just step this way!

STRATOPHANES: *You* would threaten *me*, you villain? Now I'll whittle you down to toothpicks! What do you mean coming here?

[*Cyamus defiantly blows Phronesium a kiss, which she returns*]

What's your traffic with my woman?

[*Cyamus throws a bump*]

What were you doing near my girlfriend?

[*More bumps and grinds; he draws his sword*]

You'll die this very minute unless by force of arms you prevail!

CYAMUS [*stops his lascivious dance*]: "Prevail by force of arms," you say?

[*Stratophanes' sword is at his throat. He gingerly removes it, takes a piece of string from his pocket, measures the sword and then measures his kitchen knife. With the same string, he pantomimes the sword going through his body*]

STRATOPHANES [*snatches his sword away from Cyamus*]: Do as I tell you! Stand up like a man! Now I think I will hack you up into hamburger after all. A fitting end for a cook!

[*Advances menacingly, but Cyamus stops him with a gesture*]

CYAMUS: Ah, but there's a slight catch: that battle sword you have is far longer than this kitchen knife.

[*They stop and remeasure the weapons. Stratophanes counts on his fingers*]

First let me fetch my spit from the hearth. If I have to wage war with a warrior like you, I want to do it in proper style.

[*Aside*]

A perfect opportunity to get out of here while my guts are still in place!

[*He signals slaves and makes a fluttery but silent exit. Stratophanes is left still counting inches*]

II.8

PHRONESIUM [*to Astaphium and her maids*]: Bring me my sandals. Take me inside at once. I have a headache from all this windy talk!

STRATOPHANES: *You* have a headache? And what about me? I have nothing *but* headaches to show for my generous gift of those two maids from Syria.

[*Phronesium exits; he stalks to her door*]

Gone already, are you? So that's your style, eh? How could I have been locked out more firmly than I am now? A fine trick you've played on me! But let that go. It would take very little persuasion for me to smash the anklebones of everyone in this house.

[*Turns to audience*]

What could be more fickle than a woman? As soon as she has produced my son, her pride soars out of sight. It's as if she'd said to me, "I neither ask you nor forbid you to come inside." Well, I don't want to go in, and I won't. I'll see to it that in a few days she'll begin to think of me as a rough, iron-willed brute.

[*To his company*]

Follow me! This way!

[*Turns; to audience*]

Enough of mere words!

[*Exeunt*]

III.1

[*Enter Strabax, a simple country youth whose face shows not the remotest gleam of intelligence*]

STRABAX [*bouncing a purse that hangs from his waist*]: Early this morning Father ordered me off to the country to give our cows some acorns for an early breakfast. After I got there, the gods be praised, this fellow comes up to our farmhouse and says he owes Father some money. Father had just sold him some of our Tarentine sheep. So he asks for Father. I say, "Father is in the city." I ask him, "Why do you want to see Father?" The man unties a moneybelt he has around his neck and gives me twenty minas.

[*Giggles*]

I take them gladly and put them in *my* moneybelt. The man goes away. I come straight back into town. Minus no minas, of course!

[*Doubled over with amusement at his own cleverness, he holds up the purse which dangles from his waist*]

Mars must really be angry at father dear. His sheep are not too far from the wolves now![9]

[*Starts towards Phronesium's door*]

I'll knock those city slickers out of action with one blow, and then I'll kick them all out of doors.

[*Leans forward suppressing his giggles*]

First I'll snip off Father right down to the roots; then I'll do the same to Mother. I've brought this money to a woman I love more than my own mother.

[*Approaches the door and knocks*]

Knock knock! Is anybody home? Will somebody open the door?

[*Astaphium peers out; Strabax swings the purse*]

ASTAPHIUM: What have you got there?

[*Hefts his purse suggestively*]

Why, Strabax darling! You're no stranger here. Why didn't you come right inside?
STRABAX [*shyly*]:   Was *I* supposed to do that?
ASTAPHIUM: *You* especially are supposed to.

[*Leaning on him, still clutching his purse*]

You're one of the family.
STRABAX: Here goes. I don't want you to think I'm slow.
ASTAPHIUM: Ooh, what a charmer you are!

[*They exit, Astaphium leading him by the purse; another grand pause, then...*]

III.2
[*Enter Truculentus, quite tame and solicitous*]

TRUCULENTUS: How strange young master Strabax is not home yet from the farm. I hope he hasn't somehow slipped in secret to this place. If he did, he's lost for sure.

[*Astaphium enters and sees him first*]

ASTAPHIUM [to audience]: Oh gods! If he catches sight of me, he'll start bellowing again!

TRUCULENTUS [sees her]: I'm much less savage than I was, Astaphium. I'm not the same Truculentus. You'll see. Don't be afraid. What do you say?

ASTAPHIUM: What do you want?

TRUCULENTUS: Just a little kiss from you.

[Astaphium recoils in horror]

Talk to me, order me to do anything you want. I've got a new character now. I've lost my old one. I can make love or do anything else a whore likes to do.

ASTAPHIUM [overcoming her astonishment]: What marvelous news! But tell me, do you by any chance have just a little . . .

TRUCULENTUS: . . . "money ready," you were going to say?

ASTAPHIUM: You're marvelous! You understood exactly what I was going to say.

TRUCULENTUS: Be careful! Now that I come to town so often, I'm becoming quite a suffocated wit!

ASTAPHIUM: You're becoming a what? I suppose that bit of nonsense means that you're quite sophisticated?[10]

TRUCULENTUS: Suffocated? Sophisticated? What's the difference?

ASTAPHIUM [giving up]: Follow me inside now, my delight.

TRUCULENTUS [hands her a purse]: Here, take this as a downment for bedding down with you.

ASTAPHIUM: I can't stand it! A "downment"! What kind of beast do I have here? Do you mean to say "down payment"?[11]

TRUCULENTUS: Sure, I just saved the pay for myself. Why, I even know folks in the country who can find their peckers in a woodpecker, or a dork in a stork, or . . .[12]

ASTAPHIUM [at wit's end]: Please come inside.

TRUCULENTUS: I should wait here until Strabax gets back from the country.

ASTAPHIUM: But Strabax has just returned from the country! He's inside right now!

TRUCULENTUS [flares up]: Before he even saw his own mother? What a worthless fool!

ASTAPHIUM: Now, now! Up to your usual ways?

TRUCULENTUS [thinking better of it]: Now, now! I didn't say a word.

ASTAPHIUM: Come, dear, let's go inside. Give me your hand.

TRUCULENTUS: Here.

[*She takes his hand and leads him in; he pauses and turns to the audience*]

The tavern I'm being led to specializes in gobbling up high fees for low service.

[*Exeunt*]

IV.1

[*Enter Diniarchus, transported by ecstasy*]

DINIARCHUS

No one has ever been born, or will be born,
or will ever be found, to whom I'd wish better luck
than Lady Venus! Gods above, how happy I am!
I'm swept away by happiness!
Cyamus brought me a message of pure joy:
every gift he took inside was a delight
and was accepted straightaway by Phronesium.
Even sweeter was the news of how
unwelcome the soldier's gifts were.
Pure joy, that's me! I've got the ball now!
With the soldier jilted, the woman's mine forever.
I'm saved at last, because I'm lost;
if I weren't lost this way, I'd be ruined another way.
Now to watch what goes on inside,
who comes outside and who goes inside.
I'll keep watch from here on my future fortunes.
I have nothing! She has everything! I'm at her mercy!

[*Perches outside Phronesium's door*]

IV.2

[*Enter Astaphium from house*]

ASTAPHIUM [*to servants inside*]:

I'll take care of my business out here as cleverly as I can: you be sure to do what *you*'ve got to do inside. Love what you ought to love—your own interest. Drain his pool dry. Now's the time to get his cash, while he has it, while he likes to spend it. Turn on your charms for your lover. He'll come clean if you pick him clean. I'll be on sentry duty outside as long as this fellow keeps that stream of cash flowing to your door. No bore will get inside to bother you. I won't allow it. Play your game the way you want to.

DINIARCHUS [*advances*]:   Who's being cleaned out now? Tell me, Astaphium.

ASTAPHIUM: Oh dear, it's *you*!

DINIARCHUS: Am I such a bother?

ASTAPHIUM: More than ever! Anybody who isn't of use to us is a bother to us. Now, please listen; I want to say something.

DINIARCHUS: Well, what is it? Does it have anything to do with me?

ASTAPHIUM: I won't hide it from you. Oh what hauls she's making inside!

DINIARCHUS: What? You mean there's some new lover there?

ASTAPHIUM: She's opened up a full, untouched treasure.

DINIARCHUS [*hysterical*]:   WHO?

ASTAPHIUM: I'll tell you, but keep it a secret. Do you know this fellow Strabax?

DINIARCHUS: Of course.

ASTAPHIUM: Well, he's tops with us now. He's the new crop we're harvesting. The fellow manages his affairs with a light heart and an empty head.

DINIARCHUS: He's come to a bad end, and so have I. I've got a poor return on my investment, being shut out like this.

ASTAPHIUM: You fool, you're trying to make mere words unmake what is already made.

[*Archly*]

Even Thetis stopped crying for Achilles in the end.[13]

DINIARCHUS: Then I'll not be admitted to your house?

ASTAPHIUM: Why you more than the soldier?

DINIARCHUS: Because I gave more than he did.

ASTAPHIUM: Ah, but the reason you were admitted more often was that you were paying. Now be a good sport and let those who pay get the services *they* pay for. You've learned your lesson well. Now that you know it, let someone else learn too.

DINIARCHUS [*embracing her*]:   By all means, as long as I can have a brushup lesson. I don't want to forget how.

ASTAPHIUM [*escapes*]:   What about your teacher, while you're re-

peating your lessons? She likes repetition just as much as you
do.

DINIARCHUS: How so?

ASTAPHIUM: She needs her tuition again and again.

DINIARCHUS: But I've already given today! I've even ordered five
minas of silver to be brought to her, plus one mina's worth of
groceries.

ASTAPHIUM: That's *exactly* what got here. Everyone's doing well,
thanks to your thoughtfulness.

DINIARCHUS: Oh gods, no! Are my enemies gobbling it all up? I'd
rather be dead than put up with this!

ASTAPHIUM: You're a fool.

DINIARCHUS: Why so?

ASTAPHIUM: I'll explain.

DINIARCHUS: Well, why?

ASTAPHIUM

I'd rather have my enemies
envy me than have me envy my enemies.
To envy somebody else's good fortune
when your own is down is sheer misery.
Those who envy are those who're poor.
Those who are envied are those who're rich.

DINIARCHUS: You mean I don't get a share of my own groceries?

ASTAPHIUM: If you wanted a share, you should have taken it home.
We keep our books the way they keep books in Hades: once
your account is entered on the ledger, it's on the ledger. Good
day.

[*Turns to go*]

DINIARCHUS [*holds her*]: Wait a minute!

ASTAPHIUM [*struggles free*]: Let me go!

DINIARCHUS: Let me inside!

ASTAPHIUM: Inside your own house, yes.

DINIARCHUS: No, I want to go inside your house!

ASTAPHIUM: It's impossible. You ask too much.

DINIARCHUS: Let me try!

ASTAPHIUM: No, try waiting. What you want to try is
housebreaking.

DINIARCHUS: Tell her I'm here, then.

ASTAPHIUM: Go away. She's busy. That's the truth.

DINIARCHUS: Will you come back or not?

ASTAPHIUM [as if hearing Phronesium's call]:   Only if someone calls me who has more power over me than you do.

[She goes]

DINIARCHUS: One word . . .

ASTAPHIUM: Say it.

DINIARCHUS: WILL YOU LET ME INSIDE?

ASTAPHIUM: You liar, get away from here! You said "one word" and then said five of them. Lies, all lies!

[Goes inside house]

DINIARCHUS: She's gone inside. She's shut the door. Should I put up with this? You hooker, you! Now, it's my turn to play games! I'll shout it out in every street! IT'S AGAINST THE LAW FOR YOU TO TAKE MONEY FROM SO MANY MEN! I'll turn your name over to every magistrate in town! Then I'll make you pay damages four times over. You witch! You baby snatcher! I'll expose all your crimes! Nothing will stop me now. I've lost everything I had; now I'll lose all shame. And I don't care if I look like a stupid hayseed either![14]

[Starts to go off]

But why all this shouting? What if she should order them to let me back inside? I swear I wouldn't go! Absolutely not! Not even if she wanted me to.

[Collapses]

Oh, what's the use? You can pound on clubs with your fists if you want to, but your hands will know which hurts more. Nothing comes of getting angry at nothing, not when she thinks you're worth nothing.

[Hears commotion; looks down the street]

But what's this? Ye immortal gods! I see the old man Callicles, the one who was nearly my father-in-law! He's bringing two maids all tied up: one of them's Phronesium's hairdresser; the other is one of his own slaves. I'm terrified! As if this disaster here weren't enough! Now I'm afraid all my old sins have been found out.

[He freezes in position against the wall of Phronesium's house]

IV.3

[Enter Callicles, his slaves driving two maids forward ahead of him with goad and whips. He brandishes his cane]

CALLICLES *[to his maid]*:   Why, would *I* curse you?

[To Syra, a maid of Phronesium]

> Would *I* harm you? You both already know from experience just how gentle and easygoing I can be. I questioned you both when you were strung up by your thumbs on the whipping post. My memory's sharp. I know exactly what you confessed. Now that we're here, I want to know if you'll make the same confession without punishment. You both have the cunning of a serpent, but I'm warning you, you'd better not have double tongues, or I'll cut them off for you! Or would you prefer to be led off to the clink-clank-clunk of an executioner's chains?[15]

MAID: These thongs cut our arms so. Pain makes us tell the truth.

CALLICLES: If you tell the truth, I'll have you untied.

DINIARCHUS *[in panic, to audience]*:   I don't know what's going on, but I do know I'm scared. I know what wrongs *I've* done well enough.

CALLICLES: First of all, you two stand apart. There, that's right. I'll be a wall so you won't exchange signals.

[Stands between them with arms outspread; to his maid]

> Now talk.

MAID: Talk about what?

CALLICLES: What happened to the boy, the baby my daughter had, my grandson? Outline the main points!

MAID: I gave him to her.

[Points to other maid]

CALLICLES: Now keep quiet.

[To Syra]

> Did you receive a baby from her?

SYRA: I did.

CALLICLES: Keep quiet. I don't need anything else. You've confessed enough.

SYRA: I won't deny it.

CALLICLES: Talk like that will get your reddened back time to heal over to a darker hue.

[*Aside*]

H'm. . .their stories seem to agree up to this point.

[*Reflects a moment*]

DINIARCHUS [*to audience*]: On no! Now all my deeds are exposed to public view! Everything I hoped would stay a secret!

CALLICLES [*to his maid*]: Now you talk. Who ordered you to give the baby to her?

MAID: My mistress, your wife.

CALLICLES [*to Syra*]: Now *you* talk. What did you do with the baby?

SYRA: I took it to my mistress.

CALLICLES: And what did your mistress do with the baby?

SYRA: She gave him at once to my mistress.

CALLICLES: *Which* mistress, damn you?

MAID [*volunteering*]: She has *two* mistresses.

CALLICLES [*turns on her*]: Keep out of this unless I ask you something!

[*To Syra*]

I'm asking *you*.

SYRA: The mother gave the baby to her daughter Phronesium, as a gift.

CALLICLES: You're talking more now than a little while ago.

SYRA: You're asking more.

CALLICLES [*to Syra*]: Answer me quickly now: what did the woman do who was given the baby?

SYRA: She loaned it out.

CALLICLES: To whom?

SYRA: To herself.

CALLICLES: As her own son?

SYRA: As her own son.

CALLICLES: Oh gods, I call you to witness! See how much easier it is for one woman than another to give birth to one and the same baby!

[*Gestures towards Phronesium's house*]

Thanks to another woman's labor, *this* woman gave birth to a baby boy without any pain at all. Lucky child! He has two mothers and two grandmothers. What worries me now is how many *fathers* he had!

[*To audience*]

What evils women do!

MAID [*sees Diniarchus hiding*]:   Goodness, sir, this kind of mischief is more the fault of men than women. A man got her pregnant, not a woman.

CALLICLES: I know that perfectly well enough! And *you* were such a fine guard for her, weren't you?

MAID [*assuming didactic pose*]:   "That man does more who more can do." He was a man, and he did more. He overpowered her and got what he came for.

CALLICLES: And he also got you plenty of punishment in the bargain!

MAID [*looks back at her shoulders*]:   Even if you hadn't said it, I'd know that well enough.

CALLICLES: But you haven't yet told me who he was.

MAID: I've kept quiet up to now, but I won't any longer. He's here but he doesn't show himself.

DINIARCHUS [*still standing rigidly to one side*]:   I'm turned to stone, I don't dare move. It's all in the open. My neck's on the line. I did it! It's my stupidity! I'm afraid she'll soon reveal my name!

CALLICLES: Tell me, who has dishonored my virgin daughter?

MAID [*to Diniarchus*]:   I see you! There you are, trying to prop up the wall because of your sins.

DINIARCHUS [*with eyes frozen open*]:   I'm not alive. I'm not dead. I don't know what I'm doing. I don't know whether to go up to him or to get out of here. I'm scared stiff!

CALLICLES: Will you name him or not?

MAID: Diniarchus, the man you once betrothed your daughter to.

CALLICLES: And where is the man you've named?

[*Looks about him*]

DINIARCHUS [*rushes out; throws himself at Callicles' feet like a tragic suppliant*]:   Here I am, Callicles! By these your knees do I implore, judge wisely this deed I've done so unwisely and pardon me. I did wrong only because I was out of my head with that wicked wine.

CALLICLES [*not losing the opportunity to preach*]:   It won't do to put the blame on something dumb that can't speak. If wine were able to tell a tale, it would defend itself. It's not up to wine to be sparing with men; rather men must be sparing with wine, at least men who are worth anything. But if a man is worthless by nature, it doesn't matter if he's drunk or a teetotaler: he's going to *be* worthless.

DINIARCHUS [*still on his knees, dryly*]:   Because of my offenses, I know only too well that I must listen to a great many things I don't want to hear.

[*Returns to the role of suppliant*]

I confess I've offended you, and I grant I'm guilty!

SYRA: Callicles, don't make the mistake of running an unfair trial. The defendant is pleading his case unbound, but you still have your witnesses tied up.

CALLICLES [*to attendants*]:   Let them go.

[*To his maid*]

You, go home.

[*To Syra*]

And you, too.
Give this message to your mistress Phronesium: she's to return the baby when it's sent for.

[*Exeunt; to Diniarchus*]

Come on, you, we're off to court.

DINIARCHUS: Why do you want me to go to court? *You* yourself are my judge. Indeed I beg you, Callicles! Give me your daughter's hand in marriage.

CALLICLES: Let her marry you? It seems you've already decided that point. You didn't wait for me to give her to you; you took her yourself. Now that you've got her, you can keep her. But I'll punish you with a heavy fine: a full six talents deducted from her dowry for your stupidity.

DINIARCHUS [*groveling*]:   You treat me well, sir.

CALLICLES: You'd better get back to that son of yours. What's more, get your wife out of my house as fast as you can. I'm leaving. I'll send message to that relative of mine. He'll have to find some other match for his son now.

[*Hobbles off with attendants; Syra dashes into Phronesium's house*]

DINIARCHUS [*going to Phronesium's house*]:   I'll ask her to return the baby; otherwise she'll deny everything later. Nothing to worry about, though, since she's already explained how everything happened.

[*Door opens*]

But what a stroke of luck! Here she comes!

[*As romantic as ever*]

Ah, she has a long sting, that woman; even from that distance she's piercing my heart!

IV.4

[*Enter Phronesium, sounds of a drunken orgy from inside; composes herself*]

PHRONESIUM: A courtesan who can't drink and tend to her business is a blithering fool, a cheap clay pot; the rest of her body can be pickled, but her brain had better be dry.

[*Turns to matter at hand*]

I'm really sorry my hairdresser got caught so badly. She said it's been discovered that the baby is Diniarchus's son. As soon as I heard that, I came running out as fast as I could.

DINIARCHUS [*aside*]:   What a pleasure to deal with a woman who has everything I own in the world, including my children.

[*Advances*]

PHRONESIUM: Ah, there's the sweetheart who put me in charge of all his goods.

DINIARCHUS [*sternly*]:   Woman, I've come to see you.

PHRONESIUM [*sweetly*]:   How are things, my darling?

DINIARCHUS: Don't "darling" me! Enough of that talk! I'm not here for that now.

PHRONESIUM: Goodness! I know what you *like*, what you *want*, and what you're *waiting* for: you'd like to *see* me, you want to *leave* me, and you're *waiting* to get your boy back.

DINIARCHUS [*to audience, admiringly*]:   Ye immortal gods! How plainly spoken! She's covered all the main points in just a few words.

PHRONESIUM: I know very well that you have a fiancée now, a *baby* by that fiancée, and that you have to marry her

[*With acid tone*]

and that your heart is really elsewhere, and that I'm nothing but a cast-off piece of baggage. I know you're leaving. But still, do consider, a mouse may be small, but still it's a wise little beast. It never entrusts its life to one little mousehole. If one entrance is blocked, it has another all ready and waiting.

DINIARCHUS: When I have a little more free time, I'll talk this over with you. Now give me back the baby.

PHRONESIUM: Oh, no, please, let it stay with me just a few more days!

DINIARCHUS: Absolutely not.

PHRONESIUM: Please.

DINIARCHUS: Why do you need it?

PHRONESIUM: For my personal business. Just let me have him for three days, while the soldier's being swindled. If I gain the baby, you'll gain a lot too. But if you take him away, all our hopes for the soldier will come to nothing.

DINIARCHUS [*after only a slight hesitation*]:   Well, here's hoping it works. There's no way out left for me, even if I had hoped it wouldn't work. Use the baby, then, and take care of him, since you're getting paid for your pains.

PHRONESIUM: Dear me, how I love you for doing this! Now, any time you think there's trouble brewing at your house, just run over here to my house.

[*Squeals in delight*]

A friend for the greedy is a friend indeedy!

DINIARCHUS [*resigned, turns to go*]:   Good day, Phronesium.

PHRONESIUM: Won't you call me the little apple of your eye?

DINIARCHUS: That will come up again in due course, don't worry. Anything else?

PHRONESIUM: Only that you take care.

DINIARCHUS: When I have a free moment, I'll come back to you.

[*Exit, drained in every sense of the word*]

PHRONESIUM: He's gone at last! He's left us! Say whatever you want, the proverb puts it best: you'll find your wealth where you find your friends. Thanks to this fellow, I still have a chance to get to that soldier, the one I love more than I love myself— as long as I get what I want out of him, that is. Even when we get a lot from a man, it never seems enough when we get it. That's the courtesan's glory.

[*Enter Astaphium*]

ASTAPHIUM: Shh! Be quiet!

PHRONESIUM: What is it? What's the matter?

ASTAPHIUM: The baby's father is coming.

PHRONESIUM: Let him come to me—if it really is him—let him come.

ASTAPHIUM: It's him all right.

PHRONESIUM: Then let him draw near and do just as he wishes.

ASTAPHIUM: He's right on course.

PHRONESIUM: Before this day is over, I'll have him completely snared.

V.1

[*Enter Stratophanes, dejected, with purse*]

STRATOPHANES: Here I am again, with a sack of gold for my mistress: a gift as punishment. To make her like what I've lost up to now, I've made this addition. But what's this I see!

[*Notices Phronesium and Astaphium*]

The maid and mistress at the front door. I must go to them. What are you doing here?

PHRONESIUM [*peevish*]: Don't talk to me.

STRATOPHANES: Don't be so mean.

PHRONESIUM: Oh, yes, I will. Won't you leave me alone?

STRATOPHANES: Does she have reason to quarrel, Astaphium?

ASTAPHIUM: She's absolutely right to be angry with you.

PHRONESIUM [*turns away*]: Indeed I am. The truth is, I don't dislike you enough.

STRATOPHANES: But, my delight, even if I did sin before, I've brought you a sack of gold as my penance. If you don't believe me, just look back here.

[*Holds out purse*]

PHRONESIUM [*turns away*]: My hand refuses to believe anything until it has it in it.

[*With increasing fervor*]

The baby needs food!
The mother needs it too! He needs a maid to bathe him,
and he needs a nurse! His nurse needs to drink
vintage wine day and night to have enough milk!
We need wood, we need coal, we need kindling, oil, flour,
diapers, pillows, a cradle, bed clothes for the cradle!
WE NEED INDEED THE WHOLE DAY LONG! OUR NEEDS
ARE NEVER MET IN ONE DAY! THERE'S ALWAYS NEED!

[*More calmly*]

Soldiers' babies can't be reared like birds, you know.
STRATOPHANES: Turn around and look then! Take it! This will meet your needs.
PHRONESIUM [*takes the purse but does not look at it; gives it to Astaphium after hefting it*]: All right, but it's not enough.
STRATOPHANES: I'll add another mina to this one later.
PHRONESIUM: It still isn't enough.
STRATOPHANES: At your wish, whenever you command. Now give me a kiss.
PHRONESIUM [*pushes him away*]: Let me go! I hate you!
STRATOPHANES: I can't do anything right! No love yet, and the day's nearly over. I've been tricked into trickling out more than ten talents worth of gold!
PHRONESIUM [*gives bag to Astaphium*]: Take this and put it inside.

[*Suddenly Strabax enters, drunk, from the house*]

STRABAX: Where on earth is my girl friend? I can't do anything right at the farm or here. I'm going to rot with sitting around. Poor me, I've gotten all hard lying around in bed waiting.

[*At last focuses on Phronesium*]

But look, there she is. Hey! Girl friend! What's going on?

[*Astaphium goes inside with gold*]

STRATOPHANES [*incredulously*]:   What man is this?
PHRONESIUM [*coolly*]:   A man I love far more than you.
STRATOPHANES: Than *me*? How can this be?
PHRONESIUM: This is how.

[*Turns away to Strabax*]

You won't bother me now.
STRATOPHANES: Are you going away, after taking my gold?
PHRONESIUM: I've already stored away what you gave me.

[*Astaphium reenters*]

STRABAX: Come here, girl friend, *I'*m talking to you now.
PHRONESIUM [*sweetly*]:   Ah, I'm coming to you, my deliciousness!

[*They embrace*]

STRABAX: By gosh, I mean it! I may seem dumb to you, but I want
to *have some fun.*

[*Winks knowingly*]

No matter how pretty you are, it'll be too bad for you if I don't
get to *have some fun.*

[*Winks again*]

PHRONESIUM: You want a nice hug, a little kiss?
STRABAX: I don't care what you do as long as I *have some fun.*

[*Winks again; winces of dismay on all sides; Strabax is oblivious*]

STRATOPHANES [*aside*]:   Shall I endure her being embraced before
my very eyes? By the gods, no! Far better I were dead at once!

[*In his old, thunderous style*]

Take away your hand from that man, woman, unless you
desire that both of you perish by this sword in my hand!
PHRONESIUM: Your *hand* would do well to have King Philip's coins
in it if you're so hot for love. You'll keep me from this lover
with gold, not steel, Stratophanes.

[*Strabax laughs*]

STRATOPHANES: Damnation! How can a pretty, witty woman like you love a man like *this*?

PHRONESIUM: Don't you recall the proverb the actor delivered in the theater? "Every man who's good at his trade can hold his nose when he has to."

STRATOPHANES: But how can you bear to be embraced by such...such...such a slob, such a filthy, sloppy...

PHRONESIUM: He may be filthy and sloppy to you, but he's clever and handsome to me.

STRATOPHANES: Didn't I give you gold...

PHRONESIUM: Me? You gave your *son* groceries. If you want *this*

[Gestures towards herself]

to be with *you*, you'd better have another mina of gold ready.

STRABAX *[laughing]*: You're going to hell, and how: you'd better have a coin for the ferryman at the Styx.

STRATOPHANES *[to Phronesium]*: What do you owe this creature?

PHRONESIUM: Three things.

STRATOPHANES: What three things?

PHRONESIUM: Perfume, a night with me, and most of all...a kiss.

[They embrace again]

STRATOPHANES *[aside]*: Tit for tat, obviously.

[To Phronesium]

Now, really, even if you do love him, won't you give me just a little, itsy-bitsy share too?

PHRONESIUM: What, pray tell, is it that I should give you?

STRABAX *[breaks in]*: Don't give that, even if there is any left over!

STRATOPHANES: You try to snare her with words, but I'll take her for force, my good fellow.

STRABAX: Take care you don't hurt yourself with those iron teeth of yours.

STRATOPHANES *[disgusted]*: Everyone gets in here: Doesn't matter who they are.

[Strabax and Phronesium embrace yet again]

Take your hands off her!

STRABAX: You're going to get in lots of trouble yourself, soldier boy.

STRATOPHANES: I gave her gold.

STRABAX: And I gave her silver.

STRATOPHANES: And I gave her a dress of royal purple.

STRABAX: And I gave her sheep and wool, and I'll give her lots of other things when she asks for them. You'd better use minas, not menaces, if you want to fight with me.

PHRONESIUM: What a charming creature you are, Strabax! Do keep it up!

ASTAPHIUM [aside, to audience]:   A fool and a madman are vying for their own ruin! We're saved!

STRATOPHANES: Come on, then! You go first to your ruin!

STRABAX: No! You be the first and go to hell!

STRATOPHANES [to Phronesium]:   I promise a talent of silver for you! Here are your King Philip coins. Take them.

[Hands over another purse]

PHRONESIUM: That's much better! Now join us—but see that you buy your own groceries.

STRATOPHANES [to Strabax]:   And where is your gift? Untie your moneybelt, you coarse creature. What are you afraid of?

STRABAX: You're a stranger. I live here. I don't go walking around with a moneybelt. I've brought her my flocks all tied up in this purse around my waist.

[Giggles; to Phronesium]

What a gift! I really beat him to the punch.

STRATOPHANES: Absolutely not! My gift was the best!

PHRONESIUM [to Strabax]:   Go inside now, dear, you'll be with me soon.

[To Stratophanes]

After he's done, then you can be with me too.

STRATOPHANES: What do you mean? What did you say? Me go second, after all I gave?

PHRONESIUM: You've given already, and he's going to. I have this

[Holds up Stratophanes' purse]

and I'm after that.

[Tugs on Strabax's purse]

This way both of you will be treated just the way you wanted
to be.

STRATOPHANES [*gives in*]:   So be it. As I see it, the whole business is
already finished. I'll have to take what's offered me.

[*Looks hopefully at Strabax*]

STRABAX [*indignantly*]:   One thing you won't be offered for sure is a
chance to lie in my bed!

[*They both enter the house, after much struggling to see who goes first*]

PHRONESIUM [*to the audience, with Astaphium, beaming, looking
on*]:   How cleverly I've netted them, and just the way I
meant to! I've managed this *so* nicely! Perhaps I could take
care of some of you as well?

[*Points to members of the audience*]

If anyone wants anything to do with love, let me know.

For Venus's sake, your applause!
This play was made at her command.

[*She bows; exeunt omnes*]

NOTES

This translation is based for the most part on the edition and
commentary of P. J. Enk, *Plauti Truculentus cum prolegomenis, notis
criticis, commentario exegetico* (Leiden, 1953).

INTRODUCTION: THE SLAVE WHO KNEW BETTER

1. See Cynthia S. Dessen, "Plautus' Satiric Comedy: The *Truculentus*," *Philological
Quarterly* 56 (1977): 145–168.
2. This may reflect a wordplay in the unknown Greek model for *Truculentus*,
since the Greek *tokos* means "interest" (born of money) as well as "offspring" (born of
men and women).

TRUCULENTUS

1. Unfortunately, only the first seventeen lines of the prologue survive, with three more lines after a lacuna which end with the cryptic words "Why say more?" (*quid multa?*). The problem is that for performance at least, the prologue must say more. In act 4, scene 3, Diniarchus's past sins catch up with him. Callicles enters with two servants whom he suspects of having helped Diniarchus in his seduction of his daughter; yet at that point in the play Diniarchus says only that Callicles was to have been his father-in-law (line 770) and that he fears punishment for his "old sins" (line 774). The audience has to know who Callicles is and why Diniarchus would be so afraid of him. Furthermore, in the three lines after the lacuna (lines 18–20), the prologue tells about Phronesium's deception of the *miles gloriosus* Stratophanes, and since that bit of trickery is intertwined with her conquest of Strabax and his slave Truculentus, the audience must learn the names of all three lovers in the prologue. Hence the prologue has been supplied from this point onwards with lines about Diniarchus's seamy past and the three latest victims of Phronesium and Astaphium.

2. Diniarchus's line (*re placida atque otiosa, victis hostibus* [line 75]) is thoroughly Roman in expression and sentiment, and a parody of official style. The absolute construction is typical of public documents and will be familiar to readers of Caesar's *Commentaries*. Compare the opening of a genuine public record by Pompey the Great: "Gnaeus Pompeius Magnus, general: the war of thirty years having been completed; 83,000 men having been scattered, routed, slain, and taken in surrender; 846 ships having been sunk or captured; 1,538 towns and fortresses having been received as allies. . . ."

3. According to Roman law, if one wished to have his sheep graze on public pastures (*pascua publica*), he had to pay a tax (*scriptura*) to the tax collectors and to register his flock; otherwise it was subject to confiscation.

4. Diniarchus's appalling taste leads him to proclaim in detail a cliché of ancient erotic poetry about the "sweetness" of appearances belied by the underlying "bitterness" of the mistress's true character. Compare the first-century B.C. poet Meleager of Gadara (*The Palatine Anthology* 5. 163. 3–4): "O flower-nurtured bee, why dost thou desert the buds of spring and light on Heliodora's skin? Is it true that thou wouldst signify that she hath both sweets and the sting of love, ill to bear and ever bitter to the heart?" (trans. W. R. Paton, Loeb edition).

5. Note the appropriation of the language of childbearing to the business of prostitution; this is a common figure of speech in the lines of Astaphium and her mistress Phronesium.

6. The pun on *come* and *calm* is no worse than the one Plautus contrived: Truculentus's confusion of *eira* (*ira*, wrath, in classical Latin) with *era* (mistress). He takes Astaphium to be saying *comprime eram*, "screw your mistress," when actually she says *comprime eiram* (*iram*), "check your rage," or "restrain yourself."

7. As we see in act 3, scene 2, Truculentus's Latin is far from perfect. Astaphium says *truculentus* (truculent, irascible), and Truculentus thinks she says *truncus lentus*, "sluggish, impotent hulk."

8. Diniarchus falls in and out of lucidity like a mad hero on the tragic stage, an Orestes or Heracles. He is pathological throughout the scene, and Phronesium, clinical and detached.

9. "Wolves" (*lupae*), Latin slang for "whores"; cf. *lupanaria* (whorehouse).

10. Recall act 2, scene 2. Now it is Astaphium's turn to misunderstand Truculentus, who becomes a Plautine Mrs. Malaprop. His rustic accent shortens words by a

syllable. He says "I'm a regular wit now" (*caullator* [line 683]), mispronouncing the word *cavillator* (sophisticate).

11. Truculentus drops the first syllable of *arrabo* (a Greek word for money deposited in guarantee of a contract) and says only, *rabonem habeto* (line 688), "Take this as a 'stallment" (Nixon in the Loeb edition).

12. In the original, Truculentus attributes this wit to residents in Praeneste. Praeneste, in the Alban hills to the south of Rome, is a convenient butt for an in joke about rustic Latin. "Pecker" for *woodpecker* (Nixon's version) preserves the syncopation of the original, where Truculentus says *conea* for *ciconia* (stork).

13. Thetis was the immortal mother of the mortal Achilles, the greatest of the Greek heroes to die at Troy. Her grief was a commonplace in poetry of consolation.

14. Literally, "I don't care a bit what kind of shoe I wear"; that is, he is indifferent to what social class he belongs to, since the city person wears one kind of shoe, and the rustic another.

15. Callicles is an ogre, but Plautus's audience would think him well within his rights. The testimony of slaves was judged reliable only if given under torture.

GLOSSARY and PRONUNCIATION GUIDE

Many of the names of the characters in Plautus have a meaning of their own, much like Fielding's Mrs. Slip-Slop or Dickens's Mr. Pecksniff. There is no firm rule for the English pronunciation of Greek and Latin words. Those who think otherwise should consult the entries "false quantity" and "recessive accent" in *Fowler's Modern English Usage*. The pronunciation guide is only for the use of actors and others reading the plays aloud; it is not a guide to the way the names might have been pronounced in Greek or Latin.

BACCHIDES

Archidemides	Ar-ke-dem-EE-des
Artamo ("lines," "halter")	Ar-TAH-moe
Bacchis	BAH-kiss
Bellerophon	Be-LER-o-fon
Bellona	Be-LOAN-ah
Chrysalus (cf. Greek *chrysos*, "gold")	KRISS-a-luss
Cleomachus (Greek, "renowned in battle")	Klee-OHM-a-kuss
Elatea	E-lah-TEE-ah
Epeus	E-PEE-uss
Lydus (cf. Greek *lydos*, "Lydian," Latin *ludus*, "game")	LIE-duss
Megalobulus (Greek, "high counseling")	Me-ga-LOH-bu-luss
Mina, minas	MYE-nah, MYE-nahs
Mnesilochus	Minn-ah-SILL-oh-kuss
Nicobulus (Greek,	Nie-COB-u-luss

"prevailing in counsel")
Opis (Latin, "plenty,"   OH-piss
  "riches")
Pelagon   PELL-a-gon
Pergamum   PER-ga-mum
Philoxenus (Greek,   Fill-OX-e-nuss
  "stranger-loving,"
  "hospitable")
Pistoclerus   Pis-to-KLER-uss
Sinon   SIGH-non
Spes   SPACE
Summanus   Sum-MAH-nuss
Theotimus ("honored by   The-o-TIME-uss
  the gods")
Troilus   TROY-luss
Virtus (Latin, "courage")   VEER-tuss

CASINA

Alcesimus (possibly   Al-KESS-i-muss
  "helpful" in Greek)
Casina (cf. Latin *casia*,   KAH-sin-ah
  "cinnamon")
Chalinus (cf. Greek   Ka-LIE-nuss
  chalinos, "bit," "rein")
Citrio (cf. Greek *chytra*,   SIT-ree-owe
  "pot")
Cleostrata (cf. Greek *kleos*, Klee-AH-stra-tah
  "fame," and *stratos*,
  "army")
Diphilus   DIF-e-luss
Euthynicus   Yew-thoo-NIE-kuss
Fides (Latin, "trust")   FEE-days
Kleroumenoi (Greek, "lot-   Klay-ROO-men-oy
  drawers")
Lysidamus   Liss-ah-DAY-muss
Myrrhina (Greek, "myrtle")   MEER-henn-ah
Nemea   NIMM-ee-ah
Olympio (cf. Mount   O-LIMP-ee-oh
  Olympus, Olympia)
Pardalisca (cf. Greek   Par-dah-LISS-kah
  pardalis, "panther")
Sortientes (Latin,   Sor-tee-EN-tays
  "lot-drawers")

TRUCULENTUS

Archillis — Ar-KILL-iss

Astaphium (Greek, "little raisin") — Ah-STAFF-ee-uhm

Bona fides (Latin, "good faith") — BONE-ah FEE-days

Callicles — CAL-le-clees

Cyamus (Greek, "bean") — SIGH-ah-muss

Diniarchus — Dinn-ee-ARE-kuss

Gloriosus (Latin, "braggart") — Glor-ee-OH-suss

Lucina — Loo-SIGH-nah

Mina, minas — MYE-nah, MYE-nahs

Neriene — Nerr-ee-AY-nee

Phronesis (Greek, "good sense," "prudence") — Fro-NEE-sis

Phronesium (cf. *Phronesis*) — Fro-NEE-see-uhm

Pithecium — Pith-AY-kee-uhm

Strabax (cf. Greek, *strabos*, "squinting") — STRAH-bax

Stratophanes (Greek, "light of the army") — Strah-TOFF-oh-nees

Syra (cf. Greek *Syros*, "Syrian") — SIRR-ah

Thetis — THET-iss

Truculentus (Latin, "savage," "raging") — Truck-yew-LEN-tuss

ABOUT THE AUTHOR

James Tatum is professor of classics and chairman of the Classics
Department at Dartmouth College. He is also the author of
Apuleius and the Golden Ass.

The Johns Hopkins University Press

PLAUTUS: THE DARKER COMEDIES

*This book was composed in Baskerville text and Atheneum display type by
Brushwood Graphics, from a design by Susan P. Fillion. It was printed
on S. D. Warren's 50-lb. Sebago Eggshell Cream Offset paper and
bound by the Maple Press Company.*